CAREER
COMEBACK

CAREER COMEBACK

Repackage
Yourself
to Get the
Job You
Want

Lisa Johnson Mandell

SPRINGBOARD PRESS

NEW YORK   BOSTON

Springboard Press
Hachette Book Group
237 Park Avenue, New York, NY 10017
www.HachetteBookGroup.com

First Edition: January 2010

Springboard Press is an imprint of Grand Central Publishing. The Springboard name and logo are trademarks of Hachette Book Group, Inc.

Library of Congress Cataloging-in-Publication Data

Mandell, Lisa Johnson.
    Career comeback : repackage yourself to get the job you want / Lisa Johnson Mandell. — 1st ed.
        p. cm.
    Includes index.
    ISBN 978-0-446-54965-3
    1. Career changes.   2. Vocational guidance.   3. Middle-aged persons—Employment.
4. Older persons—Employment.   I. Title.
    HF5384.M33 2010
    650.14—dc22
                            2009017013

10 9 8 7 6 5 4 3 2 1

Printed in the United States of America

To all those bold and resourceful enough
to seek a job they love

Contents

CAREER COMEBACK

If I Can Make It There, You'll Make It Anywhere

Age is an issue of mind over matter. If you don't mind, it doesn't matter.

—*Mark Twain*

Honey, you look old."

Ah, those four words every newlywed longs to hear—especially from her recently acquired husband, who is ten and a half years her senior. To his credit, he was talking about the way I looked on paper—on my résumé, to be specific—not in person. Otherwise he would have found himself sleeping in the den with the cats for the next several months. At the time we were reassessing my job search strategy, trying to figure out why the hundreds of résumés I was sending out were eliciting zero response. This was when the economy was just beginning to take a dip.

But the simple truth of the matter was that I not only looked old on paper, I *was* old. In dog years, I would be dead. I was exactly forty-nine at the time, a veritable antique by today's standards, although I prefer to use the term "classic." I was about eight months away from AARP eligibility. I was impatiently waiting at the mailbox every day in hopes of receiving my membership card so I could take advantage of all those early-bird dinner specials. And to be honest, I was at the point of needing them, because my income was minimal and my savings were dwindling. Still, that's no excuse to buy into the ageist stereotype of people over fifty lining up for early evening dinner discounts. In fact, most people I know between the ages of forty and sixty-five don't get off work in time to take advantage of them.

Looking at my situation more objectively, if forty is the new twenty and fifty is the new thirty, as the media suggest, then I was only twenty-nine, which made perfect sense; I'd been celebrating my twenty-ninth birthday for years. But when most people, particularly younger people, think of a woman nearing fifty, they envision a bad gray perm and sensible shoes. They don't envision the exquisitely cut Madonna (who is actually a few months older than I am) and they don't see a glowing Christie Brinkley. Instead they think of a wizened Dr. Ruth.

My seventy-plus-year-old mother doesn't even look like Dr. Ruth did when she was that age. As a matter of fact, some of my favorite clothes (including the famous T-shirt that was a big hit in the *Wall Street Journal* when they ran an article about me "Botoxing" my résumé) are hand-me-downs from dear "old" Mom. The former model gives me so much more than great genes—she gives me great jeans!

The fact is, age has become ambiguous these days, and last generation's stereotypes no longer apply. Still, in a workplace driven by the nation's obsession with youth, those stereotypes persist in rearing their crusty, haggard heads, stretching out their bony, emaciated fingers at those of us over forty and croaking, "Too old!" Nowadays, there are fewer jobs, and the competition for them is more fierce than ever. We certainly don't need the additional burden of ageist images and prejudices to hold us back.

Ageism is especially prevalent in my field and in my market. I'm in the entertainment industry, and I live in the youth-crazed epicenter of all things young, beautiful, and surgically enhanced: Los Angeles, right next door to Hollywood. I know my choices of profession and place of domicile are my own fault—I take full responsibility for them, as naïve as I was about their drawbacks when I selected them. I decided to move back to Los Angeles about ten years ago to better pursue my career as an entertainment journalist, to be closer to my family, and, to be perfectly honest, to have better access to a much larger pool of single men.

Through a bizarre series of events, I'd been working in Salt Lake City for the past fourteen years, where it was relatively easy to be a big fish in a small pond. But alas, I'd finally exhausted all the journalistic feeding sources: every print, radio, and television outlet in the state. I had finally become frustrated by the predominant conservatism in the area—I know, I know, it took me fourteen years to figure this out? Was I in a coma? In Utah, my editors/producers would tell me, "Lisa, we love your ideas, but could you rein them in just a little? You know how the folks are here." In Los Angeles, they'd tell me, "Love your dress, love your shoes, love your purse, love your ideas, what else ya got, babe?" The creative freedom and encouragement L.A. offered, not to mention the salaries, seemed irresistible. Then there were the men. I'd already dated every single man in a thirty-year age range from Las Vegas to Denver, and even the polygamists were starting to look good. It was high time for me to get out of Dodge.

That was almost ten years ago, and back then I didn't notice that everyone in Los Angeles was younger, blonder, and had bigger boobs than I did. I was just thrilled to be back in my own 'hood, so to speak. I was a native daughter come home. The state and its economy should welcome me with open arms, shouldn't it? I would have no trouble finding a job and fitting back in, or so I thought. My family had been an integral part of Southern California for generations! I'm one of those few people who were actually born and raised in the Southland, you see. I like to call myself a fifth-generation Angelena, because my great-great-grandparents moved to Southern Cal from Scandinavia more than a century ago. My maternal grandfather was a dean at Santa Monica City College. My maternal grandmother earned her master's at USC back in the 1920s, when most women didn't do those sorts of things, and she then worked as a junior high school counselor, helping Frank Sinatra's kids and their peers find their academic niche.

On my father's side, my grandmother owned one of those haute couture fashion salons where clothing is not displayed on racks, but rather on models—the type of place where Lauren Bacall, Betty Grable, and Marilyn Monroe worked in *How to Marry a Millionaire*. My great-aunt worked for the studios and actually costumed the great Marilyn. Aunt Susie used to entertain my sister and me with scandalous tales of the sex goddess's penchant for clothes one size too small (so she would appear to be busting out of them), and her aversion to underpants. (Unsightly VPL, doncha know?)

Rest assured that I wasn't one of those privileged, silver spoon kids who had everything laid out at my feet and never experienced hardship. We all have our crosses to bear, and I believe my trials could rival anything you've ever heard sobbed out on a talk show couch. Like most of you, I had to work and work hard for everything I'd achieved. I worked my butt off in high school to get good grades and I participated in every extracurricular activity in order to earn the scholarships necessary to get the best education available. I covered the rest of my college expenses myself—sometimes existing on one mint brownie a day—hey, if I was only going to eat once, it had to be something I loved. That was back in the late 1970s, before we started waging the Great War on Carbs, and processed sugar was still our friend.

So here I was, finally back in Los Angeles, recently turned forty and no trust fund to back me up. I was far from intimidated, however. I was a strong believer in hard work and optimism, ready to reclaim my position as a gainfully employed contributor to the Southern California economy. I've always been on the naïve side.

You see, this was the late 1990s, and even though I was a true daughter of the City of Angels with a California pedigree that stretched back over a hundred years, and the ability to speak fluent Spanish—enabling me to communicate with 99 percent of the population here; even though I had almost twenty years of journalistic experience in every aspect of the media from radio to television to newspapers to magazines and the Internet, I was in for a big surprise.

My major problem was that I wasn't twenty-two. Damn! How thoughtless of me! At first it didn't matter so much—I wrote beauty, fashion, and celebrity articles for a handful of national women's magazines, and then I got caught up in the feverish dot-com craze of the late 1990s. No one cared how old you were then, just as long as you could work eighteen hours a day, seven days a week in order to build something from scratch that could be sold off a few months after launch and make millions for everyone involved—including yourself.

Computers and the Internet were certainly nothing new to me, even back then. My first was an Apple Lisa—they named the darn thing after me, I reasoned, so I just had to get my hands on one! And I'd been on the Internet since almost before Al Gore invented it. Back when

Amazon was but a tiny trickle, I sold thousands of copies of my first book, the tongue-in-cheek *How to Snare a Millionaire*, online, and I'd been instrumental in launching City Search in Salt Lake City. So it wasn't as if, in my fifth decade, the Internet revolution had passed me by. I was constantly looking for new ways to use it—I still am. Twitter, anyone?

But during those salad days of the dot-com craze, I was also building an outrageously fun, stimulating, and marginally profitable business on the side. I became a stand-in junketeer, an insider title that doesn't sound nearly as glamorous as it is. When major studios, (Warner Bros., Paramount, Universal, Fox, etc.) release a film, they fly in entertainment reporters from the top twenty-five markets all over the country to conduct four- to six-minute one-on-one interviews with the stars of their newest films. The reporters then take the beta videotapes of those interviews back to their respective network affiliates and edit them into short news features on the stars and their movies. The studios find this coverage invaluable, because, for the relatively low price of flying broadcast journalists into New York or L.A. for the weekend and putting them up in hotels like the Four Seasons and the Regency, they get, at the very least, a two-minute feature on their film. If those pieces run several times, which they often do, and the stations also run a review, no matter if it's positive or negative, the film can be featured for a full ten minutes or more. That kind of advertising could cost the studios tens of thousands of dollars. The local stations love the fact that someone from their own staff is talking to Tom Cruise or Angelina Jolie. So everyone—the stations, the studios, and the talent—wins from this system.

Except for the poor journalists who cover these junkets every weekend. It may sound like heaven on a cracker to be flown into Beverly Hills each weekend, be put up in five-star hotels, and interview famous movie stars. But most junketeers will tell you it's great for the first six months, until it suddenly occurs to you that you're spending at least fifteen hours per weekend in transit, and every Friday, Saturday, and Sunday away from the ones you love at home. So that's where I came in. If you're a journalist who can't make it to L.A. from Boston because you want to celebrate an anniversary or watch your kid's championship soccer game, you call Lisa, and she'll do the interviews for you.

And I like to think I'm good at this interview process. As a degreed journalist, I'm skilled at doing background research and conducting interviews to get unique bites that I know will tell a great story. Since I'm not an exceptional beauty but fairly well spoken, I am unintimidating, nonthreatening, and able to put talent at ease.

I've interviewed everyone from Johnny Depp to Cate Blanchett, Steven Spielberg to Clint Eastwood. No one has flustered me yet, except perhaps for Phil Collins: We had been flown in to Disney World in Orlando to do interviews for the animated feature *Brother Bear*. Film stars such as Joaquin Phoenix and Michael Clarke Duncan, whom we also interviewed, were merely ordinary for me at that point, but the man who provided the score for this film and for my young adult life made me a little giddy.

In addition to being a good journalist, I know from film. As a good daughter of Southern California, I couldn't help but take an interest in the film industry—they're making films all around you. I couldn't resist the urge to explore the industry from the inside out. I investigated the world behind the camera, taking the occasional part-time job as a production assistant, helping with everything from lighting to craft services. I was an extra in several productions, both for the big screen and for television, and quite accidentally got featured as an FBI agent in a movie directed by Jennifer Warren, with Rutger Hauer and Paulina Porizkova (they paid me extra for appearing in my bra with a towel wrapped around my waist in a ladies' locker room scene!).

I was also fortunate enough to sell the screen rights to an unpublished book I wrote with a friend of mine from high school, and then worked with the screenwriter to complete the script. As with the majority of Hollywood projects, the movie never got produced, but my understanding of and respect for the fine art of screenwriting was infinitely enhanced. I learned how to talk to people about many aspects of the filmmaking process and come across as sincerely appreciative of their work.

So when the dot-com I'd worked so feverishly to build crashed, it seemed natural for me to segue into freelance multimedia entertainment journalism, focusing specifically on film. I was able to continue doing junkets on the weekends, and there were the occasional freelance

magazine writing jobs. Then there were some Web newswriting positions, which expanded to include blogs. And there were your sundry
Hollywood radio reporting gigs, most of which required me to get up
at 4:30 a.m. These were made infinitely easier as technology progressed
and I was able to record my reports, complete with bites from my interviews and the films, edit them together in Pro Tools, and then deliver
them almost instantaneously via e-mail in MP3 format. No more getting up at the crack of dawn for me, thanks to the miracles of modern
technology.

But put 'em all together and whaddaya got? Not enough to pay the
mortgage every month, that's for sure. What I needed was a full-time
job with a steady income, and benefits like sick leave, health insurance,
and a 401(k). I'd almost forgotten what those luxuries were like. The
uncertainty of freelancing was overwhelming, and it stifled the joy of
the freedom. I wanted one boss, rather than fifty-three.

So I dusted off my résumé and added all the new credentials I'd
cultivated by promoting *How to Snare a Millionaire* and a second book I
wrote with Bravo's Millionaire Matchmaker Patti Stanger, called *Become
Your Own Matchmaker: 8 Easy Steps for Attracting Your Perfect Mate*.

All that time I kept adding new experience to my résumé and sending it out, and getting very little response. The occasional freelance
gig would come up, mostly from friends and business associates who
knew what I could do and had extra work. But as the years went by, the
competition got stiffer, the jobs got scarcer, and the few responses I got
seemed to be tapering off.

I wasn't coming anywhere near the tasty, full-time positions for
which I was fully qualified—I wasn't even getting phone calls or first
interviews. I was, however, constantly running into the younger, hot-
ter, less experienced candidates who were actually nailing the jobs. I'd
meet them at junkets, and they'd ask me, "Where should I sit? How do
I do this? What should I ask?" Eventually, the nubile young interviewer
would bubble that she had just been hired by the very same outlet I'd
applied to several weeks before, and I'd find myself debating the pros and
cons of implants. But I often got sweet revenge on those who hired the
young, cheap, buxom, and inexperienced. They inevitably ask people
like Russell Crowe stupid, personal, and/or inappropriate questions like

"have-you-stopped-beating-your-wife-yet-boxers-or-briefs-how-much-did-you-get-paid?" He then cusses at them, throws them out of the interview room, and embarrasses both the journalist and her outlet. I can't say as I blame or hold it against dear Russell and his more cantankerous colleagues. Would *you* answer a question like that? I actually want to jump up and kiss him for that kind of behavior. Seriously, though, he's not the jerk he's been portrayed as, he just calls 'em as he sees 'em. You go, Russell!

Those types of incidents were becoming more and more frequent as media outlets seemed to be deciding that beauty and youth were more important than experience and professionalism. There was the gorgeous, fourteen-year-old-looking blonde who sat nervously in the Four Seasons hallway, wearing the most amazing pair of pink Christian Louboutins I'd ever seen. She confessed that this interview with Brendan Frasier would be her first celebrity interview ever. "Well, at least you're wearing great shoes," I told her, wondering where someone that young had come up with the funds to pay for them.

"I know, right?" she giggled. "These are supposed to give me confidence and authority. One look at these red soles and people will know I'm no rookie!" I couldn't help myself, it just slipped out: "Unless you lift your leg and scratch your ear with your toe, no one will ever see those shoes." I told her, "They never shoot your feet." Whatever happened to good old-fashioned research and preparation as confidence builders? I wondered. There are actually people out there who think high-fashion footwear is a substitute?

The stories go on. One sad lad returned to the *Dark Knight* hospitality suite looking as if he'd just spent an hour in the sauna fully clothed, rather than interviewing Christian Bale, Maggie Gyllenhaal, Gary Oldman, Christopher Nolan, and Aaron Eckhart. "Rough day?" I inquired absently, as I mentally edited the perfect sound bites from some of the best interviews I'd ever done.

"Oh man, these guys are so tough!" he exclaimed. "I'm just not feeling any love. They're even giving me attitude about my killer warm-up question. I can't believe it!"

"What's your killer warm-up question?" I asked, wondering how he could possibly start off on the wrong foot with such a diverse group of actors—especially Aaron Eckhart. He, in particular, is a softie and the consummate gentleman.

"It's a really easy question—it's about something everybody loves," the young journalist explained. "I just ask them, 'What's your favorite pizza topping?' the minute the camera starts rolling. Now, who doesn't like pizza? What's so offensive about that?"

I didn't bother to explain to him that it's ridiculously bad form and unprofessional to ask those types of banal questions. It's like asking Bill Gates what kind of laundry detergent he uses, or Michelle Obama if she prefers broccoli or spinach. It's a total waste of everyone's time.

But instances like these made me begin to question whether anyone even cared about interviews that enlighten, educate, and entertain anymore. Was everything I'd been taught in journalism school and honed over the years completely obsolete? Did anyone even care anymore about anything other than who's schtupping whom? I contemplated one of my favorite colleagues, an insanely beautiful blonde who was the star of her own wildly popular website and the ultimate fantasy of anyone with a good helping of testosterone. She had been blessed with the face of an angel, a perfect body, a razor-sharp wit, and a sweet disposition. Not only was she popular with all the studio reps and her fellow journalists, but she was superlatively admired by her demographic, those much-coveted eighteen- to thirty-four-year-old males. She got hundreds of millions of hits when her interviews appeared on YouTube, partly because she was one of the hottest women on the planet, but also because her mandate was to get the stars to drop the F-bomb. Face like a saint, mouth like a sailor. It's a combination that's unrivaled. Now, how exactly am I supposed to follow that act? I can't even write the F-word, let alone say it. It sounds ridiculous coming from my mouth— it's sort of like listening to your grandmother talk about sex.

So how was I supposed to compete with someone like that? The revelation came to me in two words: "I don't." I decided it was all about creating my own niche, just as she had filled out her own niche more than adequately. The fact that I'd recently created my own personal niche and finally found the love of my life, my first and only husband, at the tender young age of forty-seven, gave me encouragement.

I'd come up with all sorts of resourceful ways to distinguish myself from the hundreds of thousands of other single women, many of them much younger and more beautiful than I, who were all trying to attract the same men. If I could find my perfect match in my late forties, surely I could find my perfect job. There was hope for me yet!

There had to be someone out there who didn't care in the least how outrageous, buxom, or young I happened to be, or not to be. I'd even met people who didn't care about those trivialities, and had been talking to them every morning for the past several years. I had a steady gig with a great station in La Crosse, Wisconsin, where I was affectionately known as Lisa Live in Hollywood. Each morning at 6:00 a.m. I'd give those listeners the rundown on what was happening in Tinseltown, which movies were worth their valuable time and money, and which new DVDs to put in their Netflix queues. They couldn't care less what I looked like or what year I graduated. They just wanted to know which quality independent films were finally available on DVD, because the smaller films don't often make it to a theater near them. They also wanted to know which movies they would enjoy with their kids, and they trusted my judgment. Those midwestern listeners have surprisingly sophisticated taste in film, and I love them for that.

Keeping that in mind, I try to be cognizant of the films' intended audiences when I conduct my interviews with the stars and filmmakers. I wonder, "What can I ask these folks that will make my viewers and listeners feel like insiders, and make their valuable moviegoing experience that much more fun?" For me, this is so much easier than trying to figure out new and interesting ways of getting celebrities to confess their sexual secrets. My reviews and reports are distinguished by the fact that I focus on entertainment value for the time and money spent, which are major considerations these days.

With a niche, a mandate, and a mission, I renewed my job search efforts, convinced there was indeed room in the entertainment world for someone like myself. Like the numerous stars I interviewed, I would stage my own comeback—a career comeback! But there was still that one problem that my husband was pointing out to me. No doubt about it; on paper, on my résumé, I looked old. When potential employers saw my "twenty-plus years of experience" highlighted at the very top, they likely thought, "too expensive," or "over the hill." Even my husband, who is an agent and producer with his own studio and frequently goes through the hiring process, very honestly admitted that sometimes those thoughts go through his mind as he reviews résumés similar to mine.

So together we set out to "make it work," as our favorite reality host, Tim Gunn, says on *Project Runway* (one of the few guilty reality pleasures my husband and I openly admit sharing). I started my own "Project Career Makeover" program and took a series of steps that, to my total and complete surprise, gained amazing results with lightning speed. By spending only several weeks and very little cash, I was able to garner several fabulous job offers. I was turning down interview opportunities and actual positions because, after all, there are only so many hours in a day. I recouped my investment in my career comeback in the first week of full-time employment. And I did all this at a time when the economy was on the verge of tanking and my younger, hipper colleagues were being downsized right and left. I've never been the most youthful or beautiful girl in the room, and probably not the smartest either. But I can give them all a run for their money when it comes to resourcefulness, and it's that resourcefulness that I want to share with you.

Basically, my own career comeback plan involved finding my niche, branding myself, freshening up my image from head to toe, rabid social networking, and age-proofing my résumé so that my over-forty status would not be immediately apparent. I also sharpened my interview skills so that I could be ready for anything, and cool and calm under pressure.

I couldn't believe the results! Those hard-to-find potential employers ate it all up. Entercom, a major radio corporation, visited my newly created website, LisaLiveInHollywood.com, where I'd posted reviews of the latest films and interviews with the biggest stars, as well as photos of me schmoozing with them. When the hiring executive saw that, he knew I had the perfect connections to provide Hollywood content for their radio hosts. (And on radio, by the way, no one knows your age or your measurements.) Then came Digital Publishing Corp. out of Washington, D.C., which intended to start a film-oriented website. They took one look at my own blog and knew I was just the person for their project—I could hit the ground running instead of having to establish new contacts for them. They bought the blog I'd started two months earlier for several times what it cost me to launch it, and hired me to run their new website, Filmazing.com.

My radio reporting and online content creation fit together perfectly, and before I knew it, I had a full-time Web job and a part-time radio job that would run my reviews and critiques on sixteen stations in major markets—gee, how lucky could I get? Sure, I'd be working sixty-five-plus hours a week, but I was just grateful for the employment, and I could even afford to hire someone else to help me out.

So my career comeback worked for me, and I am more than willing to pass along my good fortune. Of course, I realize that most of you are not seeking jobs in the entertainment industry, and would be content with just one nice job, let alone two. Some of you may be thinking, "Cry me a river! Poor baby had a hard time getting a job watching movies and interviewing famous movie stars for a living! Let her try and find a real job that involves hard work in this economy, like the rest of us." But keep in mind that my experience can be applied to any industry or field. And hey, if I can find an ideal job in vacuous, materialistic, youth-crazed Hollywood, which has also been ravaged by the economic downturn and where all the world is younger, prettier, and infinitely more fabulous than I am, think of how much easier it will be for you in your respective fields and locations. Despite the constant sunshine, nowhere in the world, not even in Manhattan, is the professional climate as brutally cold as it is in Hollywood. Looks and youth mean everything, talent and experience count for very little. Still, there is hope, and I know where to find it. My friends, I'm here to share that knowledge with you, and help you cultivate the optimism and success you need during these very difficult times. If I can do it, anyone can.

1

Reality Check

Choose a job you love, and you will never have to work a day in your life.

—Confucius

Chances are that if you're reading this book, you're probably not at a high point in your life—you're trying to find a new job or career because what you were doing before isn't working for you anymore. At least you're in good, and ever-expanding, company! Unemployment is rising to numbers untold, many businesses are gasping and failing, and the economic outlook is a dreary shade of grim. No matter what sort of circumstances have led you to the place you've reached today, it may seem like an overwhelmingly long distance between where you are right now and where you'd like to be. If you're like me, you look around at all the world's superachievers and you start to realize that they've gone a lot further than you have in a lot less time. The election of forty-seven-year-old Barack Obama marks the first time we've had an American president who is younger than I am. That's sobering! It's easy to become intimidated, discouraged, or depressed and give in to the notion that at this point it's hopeless to try to make a career comeback. Not only is the world job market dwindling, but there's that nagging feeling that you're past your prime, and that the choices you've made up to now have led you about as far as you'll ever go.

But don't give up! You have all sorts of talents, skills, and experience working for you—or against you, as the case may be. You've developed good and bad habits and accumulated both good and bad experiences that have made you who you are today. If you're not in the exact career space you'd like to be, it's important to identify how you

got where you are and why you haven't achieved all you'd hoped, professionally speaking. By the way, never lose sight of the fact that your
career is only one aspect of your life. Personal relationships, spiritual-
ity, creativity, health, intellectual growth, and more are all important
facets of a happy life that have little to do with the economy, and that
you can control, to a certain extent. Even in these difficult times, it's
important to focus on and feel gratitude for what you *do* have, rather
than what you *don't* have.

EVEN MOVIE STARS LOSE THEIR MOJO

When I was interviewing Nia Vardalos, whom we all know
and love from her film *My Big Fat Greek Wedding*, we chatted about what was, at the time, her most recent film, *My
Life in Ruins* (which you can now catch on DVD). She played
an American tour guide in Greece whose life had hit a speed
bump—she was failing in her job, failing in her love life, and
decided she needed to rediscover her *"kefi,"* which is the
Greek term for "mojo," magic, or joie de vivre. This is what
she told me:

> I think this is something a lot of people can relate to, in
> that right now we're in a place of career crisis, financial
> crisis, all sorts of things are happening. We're coming
> out of a possible feeling of national depression, a little bit
> of "What happened?" And all of a sudden you find that
> you've lost your mojo a little bit. And it's not something
> that you know when you begin the process—you're just
> suddenly in it, or you're coming out of it, and you realize
> that it happened.
>
> I'll be honest with you. For three years I haven't been
> on camera—longer, actually, and the reason for that is
> that I lost my mojo. I came through a ten-year infertility
> battle that just punched me in the head. So I decided
> that I would just quietly withdraw from acting, and I
> would just sit in my office and write. I was going to try

and figure out what was bothering me so much. And I know now what it was. I was always taught that if you work hard, you can achieve your goals. *But you can't fight mother nature.* You can't beat something like that.

So I had to say, "I see. I give." And in doing that, I found out that there was another plan for me. I am a very happy, proud mother of a girl that I was matched with through Fost-Adopt who is so very much my daughter. [Her voice cracked with emotion here.] It's the most incredible, cosmically perfect thing that ever happened.

So I recommend losing your mojo—letting go of whatever it was you think was supposed to happen, because there's another plan for you.

You see? Your current position in life could well be one of the best things that's ever happened to you. Professionally speaking, you'll want to take a look at your life and try to discern what exactly it is that is keeping you from getting all you want in the working world. There are myriad reasons why you might not have the ideal job at this time, among them:

- I was laid off or downsized.
- I was fired.
- The job market is flooded with other highly qualified candidates.
- There are many people ahead of me with more seniority in my company, and I can't advance until they leave.
- I got divorced and need to find a better-paying job.
- Raising a family prevented me from pursuing a full-time career.
- My spouse has always been the major breadwinner but has hit some hard times, and I haven't had the need and/or desire to get serious about working until now.
- I've had health issues that kept me from accomplishing all I'd like to.
- My education qualifies me for a field that no longer interests me and I'm afraid to change at this point.

- Societal norms prevent me from trying to do what I really love.
- I need an advanced degree to pursue the field I want to go into, and I don't have the time or money to go back to school.
- I've gone as far as I can go in this field or company.
- I'm afraid to let go of a job that doesn't satisfy or challenge me, because it's too hard to find another job right now.
- I live in an area where it's not possible to make a living doing what I love.
- It seems impossible to make enough money doing what I love to do.
- I don't have the education, skills, or experience necessary to excel professionally.
- Younger people are getting all the good jobs in my field.
- I don't have enough money or resources to start the business I would like to.
- I recently found my true passion and I'm just getting started in it, but considering the current economic circumstances, my timing is off.

I'm not going to sugarcoat this. You know as well as I do that this is not the best of times to be looking for a new job. Millions are being laid off and there's intense competition for the jobs that remain. Since so many retail outlets and restaurants are closing their doors, even what some people considered "fallback" jobs are harder and harder to come by; it's no longer easy to get a job waiting tables or working retail to cover the bases until you sell your book or screenplay, get your master's degree, or make your website start paying off. And there's a new crop of younger, fresher, more energetic job seekers entering the market each spring.

But I want to emphasize that there is hope! Remember that you have something younger workers don't have—something invaluable that can only be acquired over the years. You can't buy it, you can't study and get a degree in it, no one can give it to you. You have to live it: It's called experience, and you should not underrate it. Give yourself credit for coming as far as you have up to this point, and for having the desire to go further. You're in a far better position right now than you might believe.

You 3.0

You may have heard recently of the Web moving from 2.0 to 3.0. It's a way to refer to a major upgrade, the latest and greatest iteration, a whole new technology or system. You know how just when you think you've updated your computer with the latest operating system and mastered how to use it, a company like Microsoft or Apple comes out with a new, improved version? They unabashedly market it, sending you the message that if you think Windows XP was great, just wait until you try Vista! It simplifies your life and does things you never imagined possible! Even though they might come up with something better in the next several years, you grit your teeth and buy it, because it's the best thing going right now, and you know you need to keep up.

Why not think of *yourself* as the latest, greatest edition—the best thing going right now? Your first iteration, your childhood, was You 1.0—unlike anything anyone had ever seen before, but rather primitive and raw, with lots of potential and plenty of room for improvement. When you reached young adulthood, it was You 2.0—infinitely superior to 1.0, but still with a few bugs and a lot of features left to be desired. Once you hit your prime adulthood, you graduated to You 3.0—the best version yet. You've worked through the bugs and flaws that held you back in the past, and now you've reached the point of being the finest version of yourself that the world has ever known. Remember that old commercial that said, "You're not getting older—you're getting better"? It was right!

Whether you're interested in a completely new career, upgrading your job status in the career you've already chosen, or looking for a new position to replace the one you lost, you're in a better position than ever to move forward. After all, 3.0 is your best version yet. With the wisdom and experience you've gained, the sky is truly the limit. At forty, you could well have more than half of your career ahead of you—you might have worked for twenty years, and you have at least twenty more to go. Why not use all the skills and experience you've acquired to make the second half the best half? Just in case you haven't quite embraced this idea yet, let me introduce you to Carole Santos, a remarkable woman in her mid-forties who could have been any one of us, had we made different choices. Her moving story will surprise and inspire you:

At no point in high school did I have the epiphany about college majors and career paths. By the time I was nineteen years old, I had stumbled through a couple of quarters in community college, but neither my heart nor my head were in it. Without direction and lacking specific career aspirations, the coursework was torture. I dropped out of college and took a full-time position as an office clerk in a restaurant, got married, and had two children.

I worked in accounting positions, sales and management jobs, left my first husband after he succumbed to alcohol, drugs, and gambling addictions, got married again for all the wrong reasons, and in my late thirties found myself single with two children and no formal education. Child support payments arrived irregularly, and my paychecks consistently left us with more month than money. I was angry with myself, but not quite ready to acknowledge the consequences of the bad decisions I was making.

Everything started to change when I volunteered to serve as the coordinator for my high school's twentieth class reunion, and received a disquieting e-mail asking, "Is this the same Shorecrest High School that federal prisoner Michael Santos attended?" I remembered Michael—in particular, I remembered one balmy night we'd taken a midnight stroll together. I'd heard of his arrest, conviction, and long prison sentence for selling cocaine, but I felt compelled to write, to reconnect with him.

He told me those first years in prison included thousands of hours of introspection. He wrote of his determination to grow through adversity. Michael had been in prison for more than fifteen years and he expected to serve another ten years, and during that time he had earned an undergraduate degree from Mercer University and a graduate degree from Hofstra University, and he had just finished initial drafts of his first two books. Believe it or not, this incredibly intelligent, repentant man took my breath away. From behind prison walls Michael seemed to understand me and my struggles.

My friends and family thought I'd gone crazy. People could not fathom how I could pursue a romance with a prisoner. But he told me that if he could be on a path to success, I could be too. More than twenty-two years after our moonlit walk in high school, we were married in a prison visiting room.

With his complete support, encouragement, and blessing, I returned to college to pursue nursing. With a nursing degree, I knew that I could find employment in an honorable profession near wherever my husband was confined. As a husband-and-wife team, Michael and I brought several of his books, about life within the prison system, to market. Those books generated book reviews in the *Los Angeles Times*, the *New York Times*, the *Seattle Times*, and other national news sources. The royalties sustained our family while I progressed through nursing school.

In the spring of 2008, a little more than five years after that day we were married at Fort Dix, I graduated at the top of my class and earned my nursing degree with honors. Today I work full-time as a nurse while presiding over several websites that publish my husband's work. I am financially independent, and I make monthly deposits to the account that will fund our future when Michael is released. Without a doubt, the poor decisions I made led to the painful struggles I endured in my twenties and thirties. Yet those years contributed to the woman I am in my mid-forties. I exist in peace today, with tremendous compassion and empathy for the human condition. It is precisely that depth and breadth of emotion that makes me a better wife, a better mother, a better nurse, a better person.

Carole may have gone through hell before, but right now she is exactly where she wants to be. Of course, she had to be open to inspiration no matter what the source, and she found it in the most unlikely spot—federal prison.

Our goal is to get you exactly where you want to be, professionally speaking. **It will help you tremendously to take a good long look at your life, evaluate where you are and how you got there, reassess your strengths and your values, and figure out how to combine them to move forward**. This may take some real soul-searching—it may take some professional counseling. It isn't easy to let go of the negative beliefs and doubts you've had about yourself for so long. Some people blame their parents for their current position in life: "My mother resented me." "My father never paid attention to me." Or much, much worse. Or maybe you feel a bad ex kept you from achieving everything you'd hoped. My friends, what better time to let all of that go? You can't go on blaming others for your current position. It's time to take the wheel and start driving your own life rather than letting someone from your past drive for you. In three words: "Get over it!"

Chara Gavaldon is a perfect example of getting over the mistakes made in the past, and literally taking the reins of her own life. By the time she reached her late thirties, she had two children, was twice divorced, and had spent about ten years in unsatisfying jobs that never seemed to fit. Combine that with the fact that she was raised in Mexico City by a very conservative, privileged family in which girls were not encouraged to get an education and make something of themselves, but rather to make something of the man they would marry, preferably at a very young age.

Women like Chara did not go to work in Mexico City at the time, nor did they get divorced. There were social as well as personal stigmas to deal with. But instead of wallowing in self-pity and despair or trying to find a man to bail her out, this resourceful woman looked around her, assessed her talents, passions, and community needs, and created a job and business for herself that would not only support her family, but allow them to spend ample time together. She began the "Pony Club," which gave young people from all walks of life experience riding and caring for horses. Chara had a deep and abiding love for horses and riding, and put her passion to work. Her "club" or "school" was the only one of its kind in the area, and has now served three generations of riders. Not only were her children involved, but her grandson has become a young international champion, with Chara as his coach and greatest supporter.

Her advice to other people in her situation? "Dare! Along the way you find out that many people know way less than you'd given them credit for, and that you know much more than you thought you did. At the end of the day, someone is going to do that job, fill that need, start that business. Why not you? Your imagination, ambition, and dreams are your only limits."

The Five-Piece Career Puzzle

Although she didn't realize it at the time, Chara was looking at her ideal career as a gorgeous picture puzzle made up of five interlocking pieces. Each piece was an individual aspect of her life. You'll find it helpful to assess your own career in the same way. The five pieces consist of:

1. Interests/passions. If you have no dependents or obligations, this piece might take precedence over all others. What really excites you? What are you drawn to again and again? Is there a certain subject you find yourself reading about more than any other? Do any of your friends or acquaintances have what you consider to be the perfect career? When you look through the job ads, do you see certain careers that look really appealing to you? There are actually tests that will help you assess this, like the Self-Directed Search by John Holland and the Campbell Interest and Skill Survey, both of which can be found online.

2. Skills/abilities. This piece will set you apart from your competition. What was your major in school? Your minor? Do you have an advanced degree? If you didn't go to college, in which subjects did you excel in high school? Is there something that you're really good at? Where does your experience lie? In which areas do you have special training or extraordinary experience? Which abilities always draw compliments from others? Which abilities bring you great personal satisfaction? Even if you were a stay-at-home mom, you might be particularly skilled in organizing transportation or juggling schedules, volunteerism, fund-raising, communications, etc. Any special skills you may have trained in or developed, such as computers, design, sales, management, accounting, art, sports, coaching, mentoring, etc., comprise this piece.

3. Lifestyle. This piece is all about personal preference; how many hours you're comfortable working, how late/early you want to get up and come home from work, how far you are willing to commute, etc. Would you consider moving to another city for the right job? Are you willing to travel, and if so, how much? Sometimes a job that requires you to be on the road all the time and gives you a generous expense account sounds glamorous, but when you have three months' worth of laundry piled up and your cat forgets who you are, being away so much seems less appealing. Also, you need to consider how flexible you need to be to meet the demands of others in your life. And what kind of neighborhood is the job located in? One exciting job I considered required me to file stories in an office in downtown L.A. very late at night, and that frightened me. It could be dangerous walking to my car, let alone driving home. Are you willing to work nights and weekends? Which are desires, and which are necessities?

4. Finances. This is probably the most practical piece. What's the minimum salary you can live with? Will that enable you to save for retirement as well as make ends meet? What is an attainable dream? I mean, we'd all like to be paid millions for our chocolate-tasting abilities, but what is a realistic high salary in your field? Would you be willing or able to accept a job with less pay if it truly inspired you and had the potential to lead you to greater things down the road? Are you able to accept a part-time position or an internship? How much are you willing to put up with just to have a job—any job? What about benefits such as health insurance and savings plans—are they essential to you and your family, or does your spouse have a job that covers all that? If so, how secure is that job?

5. Values. This is a piece some people think of as too much of a luxury to consider right now, but they shouldn't. It's what gives you ultimate job satisfaction. You need to ask yourself, from a professional standpoint, what is important to you? What do you believe in? Some people want a job that constantly challenges them and becomes the focal point of their lives. Others want a simple, less intense job that will allow them to save their energy and focus for their families and/or recreational interests. Do you prefer to interact with people, or are you happiest in solitude, solving problems by yourself? Are you an indoor or outdoor person? Do you smoke, and can a potential employer accommodate that? Is it important to you that your job is meaningful and contributes to the greater good, or do you get enough of that in your personal life? Is a social aspect to your job important? In other words, do you want to be friends with your coworkers, or would you rather completely separate business from pleasure?

Take notes as you consider these five pieces and how they'd ideally fit together in a job. Use the Internet to do some research. Talk to the people you know who seem to be really happy with their work, and find out why they feel the way they do. Look around your community, figure out who the major employers are, and see if they have any positions that might be a good fit for you.

A Ray of Hope

After looking at your profession in five distinct pieces, you might be surprised to find that the current profession you're pursuing is not a good fit for you—that you might be better suited to a different field altogether. Even though this may require a major life change, don't despair!

There is plenty of hope, no matter what your age or how bad the economy may be. There is probably no one better qualified to address this issue than John Challenger, CEO of Challenger Gray & Christmas, a sort of "hospital for the unemployed."

When a company stages major layoffs, they hire Challenger Gray & Christmas to help employees transition into other jobs. "Lots of companies are hiring right now," he affirms. It's just that the ones that are laying off are getting all the press. "I'm seeing more jobs in education and health care, and there are increasing subsidies for government positions in social services," he says. He adds that during tough financial times, companies that focus on basic consumer products flourish. "Everyone still brushes their teeth," he notes. The discount retail and hospitality industries are also still doing well. "People are going out, but they're trading down." For example, while high-end, gourmet restaurants are suffering, McDonald's is doing quite well, and while luxury retail establishments like Saks and Neiman Marcus are suffering, Costco and Wal-Mart are doing a brisk business.

Okay, so the knowledge that you can always get a job flipping burgers or wearing a smock with your name on it might not be too comforting, but there are many other jobs in still prosperous industries that might be more appealing to you and fit your lifestyle perfectly. For example, some industries that are currently flourishing and have some unique job opportunities include:

■ **Insurance, particularly accident, auto, and health.** Think about it; health and auto insurance are always important to people, no matter what the economy is like, and health insurance has been an important plank in every politician's platform for years now. If you drive a car, in most states you are legally required to have some sort of auto insurance. So whether you are involved in sales, claims, or administration, there will always be plenty of jobs in the insurance industry.

Don't wrinkle up your nose at the prospect—I have a friend who fashioned for himself his idea of the perfect lifestyle as a claims adjuster. He could easily do his paperwork early in the morning and finish investigating his claims, which involved being out in the community, working with people, and even doing some challenging detective work. He'd be done by 4:00 p.m. so he'd have plenty of time in the afternoon to hike, bike, ski, whatever. Moms out there, are you envisioning the freedom you would have to attend your children's after-school sporting events? And just think of the superior benefits you get at an insurance company!

■ **Health care.** Unfortunately, people are always going to get sick, even more so with the stress of tough economic times. As the largest segment of the population (Baby Boomers) ages, the need for health care increases. There is a surprising range of jobs within the health care industry—it's not just for those who love biology or working with patients. The artistic among you who are having a tough time making a living in your chosen fields can find a niche for yourselves in therapy. Art therapy and music therapy are increasing in popularity. Carl, a friend of mine in his sixties who was a performing musician for years, finally decided the late nights were no longer his cup of tea and began looking into taking daytime classes that would train him in musical therapy, which he finds infinitely more satisfying at this point in his life. He can use his talents to comfort others.

■ **Green industries.** This is the major growth field of the twenty-first century, and one of the few areas in which there still seems to be plenty of government and private funding. Anything involving biofuel, solar power, green products, recycling, etc., can't grow fast enough. There are creative and community outreach positions opening up in this field, as well as communications, sales, management, marketing, and scientific and manufacturing positions. Oh, and don't forget the bonuses that come from the tremendous job satisfaction: You would be making a real, positive difference to the entire planet! If there are no jobs like this in your own community and you are in a position where you can relocate, you might research the cities with up-and-coming green industries. Not only could you earn a decent salary, but you could be helping to save the world.

Go with Your Strengths

When I decided to stage my own career comeback, I took a good long look at myself in the figurative mirror, and I had to admit that not everything I saw was pretty. Sure, I was experienced, resourceful, intelligent, creative, and energetic. But I was not under twenty-five, and that, the most honest employers and agents told me, was the most desirable asset an on-camera entertainment reporter could have. Experience, poise, relationships, and discernment took a backseat to youth and beauty. That was the cold, hard truth. And youth was the one quality I couldn't develop, even if I felt like spending a fortune with a plastic surgeon. For a while I attempted to create my own outlets in which there would be no one to hold my age against me. I thought of an independent film show for PBS called *Inside Indiewood*. Or how about an all-female movie-critic roundtable featuring women of all ages? We womenfolk make the majority of the moviegoing decisions, and often decide what our children will see, yet most prominent film critics are male. Who wouldn't benefit from more of a female perspective? I still think those are good ideas, and maybe someone else could have gotten these projects off the ground, but I simply didn't have the juice.

I wasn't getting any closer to my goal of having a full-time job as an entertainment reporter until I stopped focusing on the fact that the industry was ageist. Rather than trying to change the industry, which of course was impossible, I decided to change my own expectations and started identifying areas in which my age wouldn't be an issue. It didn't take me long to figure out that online and on the radio, no one knows your age. I was extremely computer and Web savvy, and I had the know-how and equipment to create streaming video and audio content in my own home—that was something not every Shawn, Kim, and Mary had. Once I identified the strengths that differentiated me from all the rest, I started to make progress.

While my own experience is a little esoteric, it can apply across the board. If you're a talented jewelry maker who crafts exquisite chokers when pendants are all the rage, rather than complain about the public's inexplicable taste, use your equipment, creativity, and artistic eye to create what's hot, for heaven's sake. Accept what you can't change and adapt to what you can. Flexibility is a wonderful thing, and a very youthful characteristic, by the way.

Use Your Time Wisely

This requires being honest with yourself—absolutely, excruciatingly honest. And it just might require putting a dream on the back burner if it isn't practical. I ran into a woman recently who had been laid off from a company where she'd been employed for fourteen years, and believe it or not, she was ecstatic. "I'm not even going to think about finding a full-time job for a while," she told me. "My severance package allows me to pursue my true passion. I now have three months to write, polish, and pitch the screenplays I've always fantasized about."

After a quick intake of breath, I was on the verge of telling her not to quit her day job, but then I remembered it was too late. Here in the Land of Self-Deception, otherwise known as L.A., it seems that all inhabitants fancy themselves screenwriters. The valet who parks my car notices the studio screening parking pass on the dash and hands me a script to read on the way out. My dentist knows I'm somehow involved in entertainment and pitches me a TV series idea while he's working on my teeth. The chances of a novice screenwriter selling a script she's been working on for three months are almost nil. To be honest, the chances of a veteran screenwriter selling a script she's been working on for three years are bad enough. Spending spare time pursuing her passion would be fine for my new friend, but she should be spending an equal amount of time polishing her résumé, networking, acquiring any practical skills she lacks, and searching for legitimate job leads.

According to John Challenger, one of the biggest mistakes people make when they get laid off is not starting their new job search fast enough. "Many people spend too much time trying to figure out what they want to do, and give up the time when they're most valuable to employers," he says. Challenger adds that there are employers out there who are looking to snap up top employees just as soon as they become available, but after a certain amount of time they start wondering, "Why hasn't anyone else hired this person yet?"

Temping for an employment agency that specializes in your industry of interest is a great, productive way to spend downtime between jobs. Not only does it expose you to various aspects of your field, but it's a fabulous way to make contacts and hear about opportunities that might not be advertised on job boards. Don't pooh-pooh this idea for being "beneath you." When I first moved back to Los Angeles, I spent some time temping for an entertainment employment agency. I gained invaluable experience at studios and talent agencies, even when I was just photocopying scripts. I kept my eyes wide open and saw how things got done in this industry, and it has served me well in so many different ways.

Those of you in the field of education might consider "temping" by substitute teaching. I also did this in one of my many full-time job "hiatuses," thinking that since my grandparents, my mother, and my sister were all educators, I would be a natural. By subbing, I found out that this was not the case, and I gained a renewed respect—no, make that a sense of awe—for the educators in my family. I obviously did not inherit the good teaching gene—I was an absolute disaster with the little ones. I found that I could delete getting my teaching credentials from my dream list. In a word, I sucked!

Even the most talented actresses in Hollywood are sooner or later (mostly sooner) forced to change their game plans, find new dreams, and do brutally honest self-assessments as they "progress." **Anjelica Huston** recently told me that she has resigned herself to smaller character roles, and is more than happy to still be working and getting juicy parts like the quirky mothers in *The Darjeeling Limited* and *Choke*. **Emma Thompson** acknowledged she has an advantage living in Europe, where the films they make are more about real life, warts and all, and not so much about youth and glamour, as they are in Hollywood. Oscar nominee **Kristin Scott Thomas** agrees. She has lived and performed in France since she was eighteen, and when we were chatting about her amazing performance in the French-language feature *I've Loved You So Long*, she told me, "It's true that in French films, we are interested in 'women of a certain age.' [The French] find wrinkles and signs of experience actually interesting and exciting and intriguing.... There is space for women of my age, which is wonderful. There are a lot of grown-up films being made in France."

These über-successful and talented actresses are not raging against the Hollywood machine and trying to change the system. They have reassessed their talents, skills, and assets, and found places for themselves in which they are extremely comfortable. There is great peace and satisfaction in that. You don't see these older, wiser actresses getting married and divorced in a couple of weeks, racking up the DUIs, or participating in ugly verbal spats with paparazzi.

COOKING UP CHANGE

Paula Deen is another inspiring woman who took a good long look at herself when she was in her early forties and decided it was time to take control of her life, reassess her skills, and really make something of herself. I interviewed her several years ago when she played the part of Aunt Dora in the Cameron Crowe film *Elizabethtown*, and she talked about how she went from being a penniless, agoraphobic divorcee with two children to the super-successful restaurant owner and Emmy-winning television personality she is today. She decided to take baby steps—she wasn't comfortable leaving her home, but she was a great cook, so she started whipping up bag lunches in her kitchen and having her two sons deliver them. Eventually that business grew into The Lady and Sons, one of Savannah, Georgia's most successful restaurants. When the Food Network came calling, Paula was ready, and she now presides benevolently over her own southern cooking kingdom. Who says you can't be the next queen of your own empire?

Your Career Mission Statement

Of course it helps to really define your intentions. Dr. Nancy Irwin, a doctor of clinical psychology and author of *You Turn: Changing Direction in Midlife*, suggests creating a life mission statement to help you decide what you want to do and where you want to go professionally. She made a big professional change herself after hitting the big four-oh. She was a stand-up comedienne working a grand total of thirty minutes per night, so she decided to volunteer during the day. She worked to help sexually abused children, and from there decided she wanted to dedicate her life to educating, counseling, and advocating for children. She earned a doctorate in psychology and has a thriving practice now, specializing in the prevention and healing of child sexual abuse.

She advises coming up with your own professional mission statement by doing the following:

1. Make a list of all the things you love to do, from baking brownies to horseback riding to knitting to reading—all the things that are not only extremely satisfying but fun.

2. Make a list of all the things you'd love to do if money or time were no object, from travel to surfing to skydiving to starting a shelter for homeless animals to painting to mastering a musical instrument—all those things that you'd do if only you were younger or had more money or more spare time and didn't have to support yourself and others.

3. Make a list of the things that really make you angry—the things you'd like to change in the world or fix, from bigotry to sexism to abuse to illiteracy to pollution to poverty.

She then suggests taking those lists and connecting the dots.

You'll be surprised at the number of jobs available that can incorporate several of those items. You could take culinary classes and become an organic baker. You could work for a recreation program, teaching your skills to the underprivileged. You could get a staff job in a special department at a university that will allow you to take free classes at night. Before you even make a career change, you could volunteer in another field to see how you like it. This will also enable you to make invaluable connections and contacts when you're ready to go to work.

Irwin suggests that once you decide what is really important to you, craft a mission statement about who you are and what you want to accomplish, and make it a factor in all your professional efforts. Tape it to your mirror, put it in your purse, always keep it in mind. She gives the example of, "**I'm committed to teaching, inspiring, and making a positive difference to all those who brave my door.**" That could work for a doctor, lawyer, teacher, therapist—just about anyone. A more specific statement would be, "**I create jewelry that enhances the wearer and makes a statement.**" Or, "**I create beautiful, original letterpress materials that allow people to express themselves and communicate in an elegant, unique way.**"

You Don't Have to Be a Psychic (but It Helps!)

My friends Terry and Linda Jamison didn't find their true career path until a few years after they turned forty. They're now known worldwide as "the Psychic Twins," but they tried out many different vocations before they decided to embrace the innate talents they'd had since childhood. Now, I admit to being a bit skeptical of psychics, mediums, etc. As a journalist I've interviewed many people who claim to have psychic powers—as a matter of fact, that's how I met Terry and Linda, writing an article about them. When you're featuring psychics, the best way to find out if their powers are real is to have them do a reading on you. I have to say that the reading they gave me caused me to concede that there has to be some validity to their powers, although I don't fully understand what it is. It's a well-documented fact that they predicted the World Trade Center attacks, in substantial detail, on a national radio program back in the year 2000. The best psychics seem to have a talent for tapping into a dimension the rest of us can't seem to access. But regardless of how you feel about psychics, their story of reassessing their strengths and weaknesses to finally embrace what they feel is their true calling is fascinating:

> We took our psychic abilities completely for granted, even though as young children around the age of three we started having "psychic" experiences that included extreme sensitivity to other people, predictive dreams, and strong ESP (or telepathy). At age six, Terry named the exact number of jellybeans in a large glass jar and won first prize at the school fair. It never crossed our minds that this ability would one day translate into a career for us.
>
> We started at age twenty as professional performers—comics, singers—uprooting from Philadelphia to New York City with no training and even less experience. By the time we were twenty-five, we owned a production company, "Pop Theatrics," that produced high-end entertainment for the biggest events and nightclubs on the East Coast. By age thirty, we were appearing on *Saturday Night Live* as the two-headed housewife. Our dream was to expand our career as comic actresses in TV sitcoms and films.
>
> That dream drastically changed once we moved from New York to Los Angeles a few years later. Adult "twin" jobs of any kind were not just scarce, they were nonexistent. Whatever happened to the Doublemint Twins? Remember the slogan "Which twin has the Toni?" We just missed that phase. The Olsen twins were about four years old; we, on the other hand, while still "cute," were pushing forty. While honing our stand-up act at the Improv, we realized we'd better have something to fall back on, and we began quietly and deliberately developing those innate psychic talents that had manifested themselves so long ago.
>
> It took extreme commitment, but our careers evolved. Along our journey, we encountered rampant sexism, ageism, and enormous prejudice from people who had little grasp of the paranormal. We quickly realized that our job was to create a bridge of understanding to help people learn about this

mysterious and mystical realm, to shine a beacon of hope and inspiration in a dark world.

In our forties we used the skills we'd honed as entertainers, along with our natural psychic abilities, to give birth to "the Psychic Twins." To our great surprise, Hollywood producers started showing an interest in our psychic abilities! They asked us to do medical intuitive work, celebrity predictions, and readings live on TV. We are not, after all, your grandmother's psychics with their tarot cards and smokers' voices. We eventually landed guest spots on more than sixty major network TV shows. We starred in a dozen documentary films. Now we're in our early fifties, and it seems that every day some new and exciting opportunity comes our way, many in the form of helping comfort those in need. There are a lot of people out there now who need comforting.

We found we had a special gift to motivate, inspire, and counsel others, especially women, through our psychic abilities. It came down to what we call the three R's: Reinvent, Refocus, and Restore faith in ourselves. If you have talent, you must believe in yourself or no one else will; and you must take extraordinary action toward your goals. It is about finding your authentic self.

Extra Help in Finding Your Perfect Career

Those of us who are a little less spiritually inclined and have no psychic powers whatsoever might find that the services of a career coach or counselor would come in handy. These professionals will charge a fee to help facilitate your job search. Finding a good career coach or counselor is a bit like finding a good therapist: Get referrals from your friends and colleagues, search the Internet, and chat with a number of them until you find a good fit. Don't automatically lean toward the "nicest." You do want someone who will be supportive, but you want them to tell you the truth, even if it hurts a little. We all can use a firm but gentle kick in the butt on occasion, and a good career coach will do that.

GETTING FIRED UP

ABC News career expert Tory Johnson offers amazing professional advice and career counseling services through her books and the company she founded, Women for Hire (WomenForHire.com). Formerly an executive in the entertainment industry, she had her own epiphany when she was fired from a major corporation, and she went on to become the only producer of high-caliber recruiting events for women. At WomenForHire.com, she posts invaluable and thorough job search information for women at all stages of life and gives people the opportunity to sign up for her Career Boot Camps, which are held in various cities. If you have the funds to get involved in a Boot Camp, you'll find it well worth your while.

Laura McGreevy, president of Personnel Profiles of Kentucky, is another career counselor who knows about career comebacks from personal experience—she's staged several career comebacks of her own, building on her experience and education in psychology, human resource management, sales and sales management, recruiting, and staffing. It wasn't until she reached her early fifties, however, that she found her current and abiding passion—helping people find jobs they love, and helping businesses hire, engage, and retain top employees. She uses a combination of mental aptitude and personality assessments, as well as technology, interviewing, coaching, and other tools. She says the cost to an individual who comes to her for career assessment and counseling is usually in the $250–$350 range, and includes interpretation of the Myers-Briggs personality test, as well as counseling.

Laura says the most common issue her clients bring to her is fear, pure and simple. They worry, no matter what their age, that it may be too late to start over or to accomplish very much. One way to get past this, she advises, is to stay current and to learn new technologies. Practicing what she preaches, she's now in her early sixties, keeps her iPod up to date with the latest music, and is in the process of switching from PC to Mac.

Another way Laura suggests to get over your general fear, sharpen your current professional (and social) skills, and make exceptional contacts is to volunteer. Volunteer organizations usually offer a nurturing, less intense environment that can build confidence. She notes that it has not always been easy for her to get up and speak, to make contacts, and to mentor, but gradually she reached the point where she has become a leader in professional organizations like the Society for Human Resource Management and the Northern Kentucky Area Workforce Investment Board, as well as in charitable foundations such as Welcome House, a nonprofit organization that aids the homeless, and the "I Have Wings" Foundation, a nonprofit breast cancer organization founded by her sister. She notes that there was a time when she could barely help herself, but she has managed to put aside her own personal fears and reach a position where she can help many, many others. A career coach who has persevered through her own professional challenges is a very good choice.

Whether you hire someone else to coach you or decide to go it alone, you can't help but be up against some very stiff competition of all ages now, in the current depressed job market, more than ever. It's important to be aware of your competitors' strengths and weaknesses as well as your own. The next chapter will give you some very strategic advice and information on that.

2

Know What You're Up Against

You are as young as your faith, as old as your doubt;
as young as your self-confidence, as old as your fear;
as young as your hope, as old as your despair.

—Douglas MacArthur

The job market is not a pretty place right now. As a matter of fact, it's a jungle out there, and not the lush, pretty tropical kind. There are man- and woman-eating predators around every corner, in every cubicle. Now more than ever you'll be facing the stiffest of competition not only to land a new job, but also to hang on to your current one or to secure a promotion. Even if high unemployment rates weren't an issue these days, any job or business worth having is going to be a hot commodity, and there will be others who want it just as much as you do. In addition, I hate to tell you this, but if you're staging a career comeback, it's highly likely that your competition will be younger than you are. While Baby Boomers are beginning to retire and vacate the workplace, those in Generation X are trying to claw their way to the top, and those in Generation Y are flooding the job market, attempting to get a foothold and establish themselves.

I can't tell you how many times I've walked into a reception area, decked out in my finest attire for a job interview, and been surrounded by girls who are younger, prettier, and more chicly dressed than I am. My imagination starts jumping hurdles: "She doesn't even look like she's been out of college long enough to earn the money to buy that Prada bag...it's obviously a graduation gift from her parents...her wealthy parents...her wealthy and influential parents...I bet her dad plays golf with the executive vice president of this company...she's already got the inside track...oh my god, the rest of these interviews are probably just a formality...I'm only here so they can comply with state employment requirements..." and I've almost psyched myself out of the job before they even call my name for the interview.

I wish someone would have informed me when I first started my own career comeback that as we age, we have some distinct advantages over those in succeeding generations. Unfortunately, we also have some disadvantages. But if we know what they are, we can downplay the negatives if not eliminate them altogether. And knowing the strengths and weaknesses of other generations can also work in our favor. Not that we want to point out how inept they are and how capable we are, but it never hurts to focus on our strengths—the contrast can go unspoken, but will still be blatantly apparent. For example, those in Generation Y are notorious for texting their friends, sending instant messages, and checking Facebook on company time. Without pointing that out, you can say something like, "I like to leave my personal life outside the office and put my full focus and attention on the job at hand. I stick with a project from start to finish, and I'm not easily distracted." Statements like those are music to a potential employer's ears.

So let's explore the pros and cons of each generation we'll encounter in the workplace. The more you know about your competition, the better you'll be able to exploit their weaknesses. Ooops! Did I just write that? I meant, the more you know about your competition, the better you'll be able to compete. First, a definition of the generations, and a little about how the cultural influences they grew up with affect them in the workplace:

The Silent Generation: Those born before 1946. Many were around during the Depression and World War II. They respect authority, work hard, and often believe that work is work—it isn't fun, it isn't play. They are extremely loyal and do not embrace change easily. You've probably heard at least one of them mutter, "We do it like that because that's the way we've always done it and we're not going to change now."

The flip side of this rigid attitude is that they value industriousness and loyalty, and liberally reward it. Since the majority of this generation are well into their sixties, seventies, and even eighties, many have retired or reached their peak in the workplace. But don't count them out yet—they are far from over the hill. They can serve as invaluable mentors, and they could well be the ones with the last, ultimate, and final word on salary, hiring, and promoting.

Baby Boomers: Those born between 1946 and 1963. There were approximately 84 million births in the United States during those years, more than during any other period. They were probably raised with discipline by the Silent Generation, and, as a knee-jerk reaction, they're likely to be a little more relaxed with their kids, who are probably late Gen X or Gen Y. They don't want their offspring to experience the hardships they did as they grew up, so they tend to spoil their children a little.

They were aware of, and might have even participated in, the sexual revolution, the struggle for civil rights, and the Vietnam War. They are the first generation to have divorced parents as the norm. They are more loyal to their profession than to their specific employer—for example, if a Boomer is a teacher, she'll switch to a school where she feels she can better use her talents and experience rather than stick around the same school for her entire career in order to build up seniority, as a member of the Silent Generation would. Because Boomers had so much competition and had to work so hard to stand out, they resent slackers, and are willing to stay late and work weekends to finish the current project.

Generation X: Those born between 1964 and 1979. They are also known as "Baby Busters," because of the decrease in births after the Baby Boom. There were approximately 48 million babies born in the United States during those years. Even though Baby Boomers far outnumber them, they are the ones nipping at Boomers' heels at work, and they are the ones most likely to try and take a Boomer's place.

As they grew up, they were influenced by *Sesame Street*, MTV, and Reaganomics. They were the first generation to embrace popular culture as their predominant culture. Many of them were latchkey kids, left on their own while both parents worked, and as a result they value independence and distrust authority. This makes them very entrepreneurial. In a conventional work environment, they often resent the vast number of Baby Boomers who came before them and whom they perceive to be clogging the system.

Generation Y: Those born between 1980 and 1995. There were approximately 70 million births in the United States during this time period, which accounts for them outnumbering those in Generation X and literally giving Baby Boomers a run for their money. Since there are so many of them and they are still young and impressionable (not as set in their ways or brand loyal as their elders tend to be), they are the demographic most coveted by advertisers, and therefore most catered to by the media. Ever wondered why everyone you see in the media is so young and beautiful, and so many television shows seem geared toward nineteen-year-olds? That's why.

They have been most influenced by the terrorist attacks of 9/11 and the shootings at Columbine. These are also the children raised to believe that everyone is special, that everyone's a winner, and it's important just to be you. They hardly remember life before the Internet and cell phones, and are, as a whole, extremely tech savvy.

They are used to media saturation and immediate gratification, and generally have very short attention spans. In the workplace, they want to be challenged and complimented constantly. They are very open to change; in fact, they thrive on it. They are also consummate multitaskers.

Millennials: You often hear those who enter the workplace from 1999 on referred to as Millennials. They have most of the same characteristics as those in Generation Y.

Fun Fact

There will be a severe labor shortage by 2010 as Baby Boomers begin to retire.

You Mean Our Parents Were Right?

If you're over forty, and most of the people reading this book probably will be, think about the values that your parents, who were most likely of the Silent Generation, taught you. They made you stay inside and finish your homework before you could go outside and play. They made you practice the clarinet you begged them to rent for you. And even if you were getting pounded every week at volleyball practice, they made you stay on the team because no one likes a quitter. You thought your parents were the meanest people on earth.

Now think about the messages kids have been getting from their parents for the past twenty years or so. Because Silent Generation parents were so darn strict, a Boomer's likely reaction is to be more relaxed. "The teacher is giving her too much homework. A kid needs time to be a kid," they say. Or, "Once music lessons or volleyball practice stop being fun, it's time to quit." And, "Who cares about perfect attendance? Sure you can skip school to go to the beach—it's a beautiful day, there will be fewer crowds, and after all, it's an educational experience!" Many young workers have been raised to believe that not much is their fault and that the blame lies elsewhere, because after all, *they* are special! You might hear them say something like, "Macs are such crappy computers!" when what they really mean is, "I'm more used to working on a PC and have limited experience with a Mac, so I don't know how to make it do what I want it to." Or, "It's my roommate's fault that I'm late today—she kept me up all night and I didn't get any sleep." A more seasoned employee takes responsibility and makes adjustments to arrive at work on time, knowing that she can't blame anyone else for her own behavior.

Although many Boomers resent their parents for being too harsh and strict with them, if they take a few steps back, they'll see that that wasn't such a bad thing. Chances are you know someone like my husband, James, a Baby Boomer who can sit down at a piano and play anything you ask, from classical to standards to pop. It became apparent that James was something of a music prodigy at a very early age. Realizing this, his father, who was of the Silent Generation and a great music lover himself, was overjoyed, and enrolled him in a number of very rigorous musical training programs. He also trotted his son out to perform whenever they had company. Sometimes James resented his dad, who made him sit at the piano for hours each day while his friends were outside playing ball. He missed out on field trips and games and sleepovers because he had to attend concerts and competitions. Once he graduated high school and began attending the New England Conservatory, however, he became infinitely grateful for his father's "cruel" discipline, and he still is to this day. He had a fascinating career as a professional musician and was a recording artist with a major label for several years. While he plays mostly for his own enjoyment now, the tenacity and dedication he learned as a professional musician enabled him to build his current business up from scratch. And he's still using his musical talent and remarkable ear at his voiceover talent agency and production studio. There isn't one day that doesn't go by when he isn't grateful for the dedication and skill he learned as a child.

Fun Fact

Over the next two decades, the American Society of Training and Development predicts that 76 million Americans will retire. Only 46 million will be arriving to replace them. Most of those new workers will be members of Generation Y.

The attitudes and values we were raised with can't help but show up in our professional demeanor. Generation Y was raised with the media telling them that they are all special no matter what they do. It was the fashion to give everybody on the soccer team a trophy, whether they scored dozens of goals or sat on their butts and picked dandelions. That sent the message that there's no such thing as a loser or a failure. That message may be great for the old self-esteem, but translate that to the workplace and you find some people who believe that when something goes awry, it must not be their fault, because they can do no wrong.

Of course, many employers feel that younger workers' lack of willingness to take responsibility for their actions is more than compensated for by their advanced technology skills. This is further testament to the fact that those over forty cannot rest on their work-ethical laurels. If they want to compete with Generation Y, they'd better learn to use the damn computer and all its corresponding technologies, and fast!

Still, the generation that raised us even affects the way we communicate in the workplace. In researching this book, I got my hands on some super-secret human resources documents from one of America's most prominent corporations. Chances are you have a number of their products in your home right now. Of particular interest to me is the way they counsel managers to communicate with their workers from different generations. I've summarized it below:

HOW TO COMMUNICATE WITH . . .

Baby Boomers: They prefer to keep business discussions concise and focused, without personal, non-work-related embellishment. Personal matters can be discussed after hours, outside the workplace, or on breaks. They believe important matters should be discussed face-to-face, with second-tier issues discussed over the phone. They are acutely aware of body language and eye contact, and often read physical signs and cues for the subtext of the message being conveyed. Diplomacy is respected and cultivated. Praise is appreciated but not constantly expected, and best received accompanied by a reward, such as a raise, promotion, or bonus. When it comes to written communication, they usually pay strict attention to punctuation, spelling, and grammar, as they were taught in their English classes.

Generation X: They also like to get straight to the point and often start thinking about the solution before the problem has been completely laid out. Time is of the essence with them. They are perfectly comfortable communicating in person, over the phone, or via text and e-mail, with the latter being their preferred method. They're exceptionally good at organizing their e-mails and keeping track of them. They know the value of having a record of every communication. That being said, they are not uncomfortable with face-to-face communication of important matters. Micromanagement drives them crazy. They are best incentivized by laying out goals with results that can easily be measured in a relatively short amount of time. Look for their written communication to be fairly accurate and concise, because they've mastered the fine art of spell and grammar check on their computers.

Generation Y: Business communication is best conducted with them via text or Twitter, and by traditional e-mail if the former options are not available. Most believe face-to-face interaction is for socialization, and will insert distracting personal information into business discussions. They respond well to immediate feedback, and are willing to give it as well as receive it. When communicating with them in person, don't expect eye-to-eye contact—they could be glancing down as they text or tweet while you're talking, and often text and surf the Web during meetings, which is not always a bad thing as it sometimes renders the freshest information available at that very second. Their written communication is often awkward unless it's in text shorthand—they use that so much that many forget how to spell and punctuate properly. They do not appreciate having their spelling or grammar corrected, as they feel that this is an old-fashioned way to communicate and hinders them in getting their important points across.

Fun Fact

Gen X and Gen Y far prefer texting to e-mail or talking on the phone. They also use the Internet as their preferred news source. Watching shows online is rapidly gaining in popularity over watching shows on television. Social networks like MySpace and Facebook are very important to them—more so than groups that have physical meetings. Recently, social networking sites have surpassed all others in terms of traffic and popularity.

Technology has changed everything in the past ten years, and will probably change everything again in the next ten. Today you see a seasoned CEO who has been rendered utterly useless for the past three hours, being humiliated by having to surrender his large executive desk to the twenty-four-year-old IT expert who can fix the computer glitch in thirty seconds. Because of this, it may seem that Generation Y workers are poised to take over the world, but know that they are not without their weaknesses.

Generalities About Gen Y

Even though they may seem extremely threatening, remember not to be too harsh on these "kids," since they'll be the ones contributing to your Social Security and Medicare funds when you start needing them. However, many articles have been written about the *perceived* shortcomings of Generation Y:

They're lazy. They often arrive late, and take inordinate amounts of time off. A broken fingernail is a medical emergency, and a late-night drinking binge requires a personal leave day. Their response to this is that they work quicker and more efficiently when they're on the premises (which they often do), and that their priorities are different from their elders: They don't allow their jobs to rule their lives, but prefer their lives to rule their jobs.

They're not loyal. Rather than stay with one firm, they flit from job to job, whatever is coolest and hippest at the moment, wherever they can get the most time off, or wherever they can do the most socializing with their friends. In their own defense, they say that companies today show no loyalty to their employees and are likely to lay them off in a heartbeat, so why should employees be loyal to them? They all know someone their age who has been laid off or downsized, and they believe that quitting before they get fired looks better on the résumé.

They have a sense of entitlement. This attitude is cultivated by their parents and by the media. Everyone on TV wears designer clothes, drives expensive cars, and has all the latest technological gadgets, so why shouldn't they? Their parents, both of whom probably worked and spent little time with them, tried to assuage their parental guilt by giving their children material goods. Since they've always had the best, they expect immediate salaries that will provide those luxuries for them. They've been told that everyone is a star no matter who they are, and they expect to be treated like one.

They have unrealistic expectations. They've seen so many movies and TV shows about the little guy going from zero to hero in a mere two hours, they expect to be able to do the same. Even Jack Black's tubby slacker Kung Fu Panda took only about two weeks to race ahead of and become the leader of a group of martial artists who had been studying and disciplining themselves all their lives. Many workers in Generation Y expect to be promoted to upper-level in a very short time, just because they're late only once a week. Being a go-getter is one thing, but expecting the proverbial gold star just for showing up is another.

They need constant feedback and praise. "Mom, Mom, look at my pretty picture!" "Dad, Dad, watch me! Watch me!" Their parents gave them a lot of attention when they were with them, and they expect the same thing from their superiors at work. Remember how you used to tell your kid that his picture was beautiful, even if it was a scribbled mess? You weren't doing him any favors.

They wear inappropriate attire. Believing that how you look is not as important as how you perform, and that dress is an invaluable form of self expression, you'll sometimes see younger males coming to work in baggy shorts and frayed T-shirts with obscene slogans, while females saunter in in halters with dangerously low-slung jeans and muffin tops protruding. This is tricky, because they know that if someone complains about this, they can accuse them of being "out of it," a lech, or just plain jealous. They resent being asked to groom themselves with more care.

Pam, a forty-six-year-old college professor who teaches computer science classes in Colorado, says, "I have definitely seen a change in the students in my classes. The younger students [age twenty-two to twenty-nine] seem to want more information spelled out for them, and they are less likely to work long hours to figure things out. If they don't get it in the time they assumed that they would have to spend, they give up. Not a good fit for the computing field, where you can never predict how long it will take to troubleshoot something. Of course, our enrollments in computing are at an all-time low in America, because the younger generation sees the field as 'too hard' and 'too geeky.'"

Just Because You're Older Doesn't Mean You're Better

If those of you over forty are feeling pretty smug right now, it's not exactly time to start pricing that beach condo you're going to buy with your newly exorbitant salary. In all fairness, those of us over forty have a few perceived faults of our own. A number of studies have been done that show that younger workers often attribute what they consider to be their parents' flaws to workers of their parents' age. And to tell you the truth, in my case at least, I'm surprised at how many of these shoes fit, so to speak. I've displayed every negative trait on the list to some degree, at one time or another. Being aware of and sensitive to these common complaints about your generation will help you to eliminate them—or at least hide them really well. Take a deep breath now, and tighten those stomach muscles, because some of these are really harsh, and are bound to hit you where it hurts. This is what Generation Y thinks of workers ten years ahead of them:

You don't listen. You feel you already know all the answers and you've been there, done that ad nauseam. Your minds wander to similar experiences in the past, so you're not giving full attention to what's happening right now. And you don't give credence to the things "young whippersnappers" are telling you.

You don't follow directions. Since you feel you've already done everything several times and have so much confidence in your ability to get the job done, you don't see the need to follow new directions, especially when they're given by younger workers, who have watched their parents too many times try to put things together without even reading the instructions.

You're a slow learner. The saying that you can't teach an old dog new tricks is true. It's a biological fact that brain cells degenerate as you age, and age-related conditions like Alzheimer's and dementia can start creeping up on you when you're in your forties.

You're not as motivated. A lot of you are just biding your time until retirement, trying to fly under the radar and keep your job just long enough for the Social Security payments and retirement bonuses to kick in.

You don't adapt well. You're uncomfortable with change, and prefer doing things the way they've always been done. You know what you like and are unwilling to try anything new. You prefer the tried and true rather than the new and different. The unfamiliar makes you uneasy.

You're technologically obsolete. Your technology skills, if you have any, are outdated. You have no clue about how to use a computer, the Internet, or the latest communication devices. You probably don't even text or tweet.

You're more expensive. You expect employers to compensate you for all those years of experience, regardless of whether or not that experience applies to the job at hand, or pays off for the company. Because you've been in the workforce so long, you've reached a certain salary level and you won't go beneath that. Two or three younger workers could probably be hired for the same amount of money they pay one person your age.

You're unwilling to mentor. You don't want to train your own replacement, so you guard your time and experience like they were the crown jewels. You figure you'll let younger workers suffer and learn from their own mistakes, rather than benefit from your experience. After all, you had to muddle through on your own, why shouldn't those who come after you? You're worried about us learning too quickly and surpassing you.

Don't Be "That Woman"

Melissa, a twenty-four-year-old social services worker with a master's degree, works for a nonprofit organization that helps underprivileged and abused women get back on their feet. I truly admire the path she's chosen, and listened carefully when she told me that sometimes stereotypes about older workers are valid:

> "One of my colleagues is constantly asking me to do her computer tasks for her. Each time I tell her I would be happy to teach her how to do them herself, she just laughs and says she could never learn those types of things, and that it's so much easier if I do it for her. She refuses to learn. She's also constantly taking time off to deal with family issues. She has kids in high school and aging parents, and takes off at least one afternoon per week to take care of some family emergency. I understand she's needed outside the office, but she's needed inside the office too, and we really can't depend on her. I'm young, single, and have no children. It doesn't seem fair for me to be penalized with extra work because she has a family and I don't. Sure, she has seniority here, but we're at an equal level, and I shouldn't have to do her job for her. There have been times when I have to work fifty hours a week so she can work thirty."

So What Have They Got That We Don't?

Perhaps even more important than knowing the weaknesses of other generations is knowing their strengths. It would serve you well to brush up in these areas. You might not have time to get to a level where you can go toe-to-toe with them, but at least they won't leave you in the dust. Brace yourself, however. In some ways, looking at their strengths in the workplace will feel a lot like looking at the nubile young twenty-four-year-old in the dressing room at the gym. She has long, cellulite-free legs, a perfectly flat stomach, perky breasts, and thick, shiny hair without a trace of gray at the roots. Makes you want to vomit at first, and you silently exclaim to yourself, "Oh my God! I am so not renewing my membership here!" (Although my generation probably wouldn't say, "so not...") But after that initial, queasy reaction, you take a deep breath and start to realize that with a little work, you can look like that too.

Strengths of Gen Y

They're extremely tech savvy. Their lives are devoted to seeking out the latest and greatest, and being the first to adapt to it. That really cool application you just heard about? It was obsolete to them last month. They grew up with computers and the Internet. They are definitely up on all the cutting-edge technology, and there will be times you'll just have to acknowledge their superiority in that field, smile, and say, "Could you show me how to use that?" Buy them a latte for their efforts and they'll be your new best friend.

They're quick learners. Their short attention spans serve them well in this area—they find something new to learn every two minutes. They embrace it, ingest it, make it part of their core of knowledge, and move on to the next new thing before most of us can delete our spam. This is one of the reasons they feel justified in working shorter and fewer hours. They cram an obscene amount into the hours they do work—and fuel it all with mind-exploding amounts of caffeine. This is the generation that went from mother's milk to Red Bull and quadruple espresso shots. I don't know about you, but it makes me tired just thinking about it.

They're not mercenary. This will surprise you. Mom and Dad have given so many of them so much that they're now more interested in meaning than money. If they're lucky, they already have their Louis Vuitton bags and BMWs, so at this point it's very important to them that their jobs have social or environmental significance, and they will sacrifice high salaries for a cause they believe in (many of their parents will supplement their income to make themselves feel better about their own jobs). Their after-hours life is far more important to them than their working life, so overtime pay is not always an incentive. They would rather leave what they consider high-paying grunt work to someone else.

They're green. So many employers feel guilty about not being more environmentally correct, but don't have a clue about how to realistically adapt green practices in the workplace. So they hire a fresh, young, idealistic employee to help them become more aware and turn things around. They know how to cut costs and avoid waste, so they're good for the bottom line. Just having a recycling bin in the break room is no longer enough.

They're highly adaptable. Again, their short attention spans make them extremely receptive to change, and they consider it a fun challenge to embrace new environments, technologies, management structures, even lunch menus in the cafeteria. They are chameleonlike, and hardly even notice that they are changing, while the rest of us are groaning because we just got used to the last system and now we're getting a new one. It seems that the younger they are, the more flexible they are—just ask the Chinese gymnastics coaches.

They're masters of multitasking. While they're calling good morning to you from their desks, they're simultaneously texting a supervisor, running numbers on their computers, and listening to a financial trends report they downloaded that morning on their iPod. No one multitasks like a Gen Y'er. You might think they're not listening to you while their heads are bent over their BlackBerrys and their thumbs are pecking, but they're actually getting twice as much work done as you are.

Actually, being beaten out for a job by younger, cheaper candidates is not always a bad thing. Steve Oldfield, who—if you live anywhere near Cincinnati—you've seen on Fox's WXIX, credits ageism as being instrumental in helping him find his true passion: teaching.

> When I was in high school, a motivational speaker gave me advice I've carried with me throughout life: "Never make someone else's strengths *your* weaknesses." I should be happy about what I could accomplish and not be intimidated or discouraged by others' talents or successes.
>
> In an ultracompetitive career like television news, that advice served me well for two decades. I may not have the deepest baritone or the chiseled jawline of some of the other anchors and reporters, but I was always confident in my ability to tell a story and to handle any kind of "live" situation. I happily became a "news nomad," moving seven times in twelve years, working in some respected newsrooms in Orlando, Miami, and Los Angeles. I was so caught up in chasing the mythical "ultimate broadcasting job," I didn't realize the business was changing—and fast!
>
> When I moved back home to care for my aging parents, I considered the Cincinnati market far inferior to the larger places where I'd succeeded. I figured the local affiliate would be thrilled to have a veteran reporter with major-market and network-level experience. Boy was I wrong! While struggling to make ends meet as a part-time reporter, I was passed up for full-time work by people with much less experience. That's when it hit me: Their strength was their *age* and willingness to work for less money than someone with my level of experience would command. Those "strengths" definitely *were* my weaknesses. I realized it was time to find another career to at least supplement my meager part-time earnings at the television station.

I come from a long line of teachers and always had figured that's how I'd spend my late fifties into retirement. I hadn't planned on moving into teaching at the age of forty-two; but that seemed like an infinitely better option than supplementing my part-time television work with something like a job at a call center.

Even though I didn't have my master's degree or a teaching credential, I decided to take a stab at teaching by making an appointment with the headmaster of the private high school from which I graduated. Luckily, he remembered me and told me he had been watching me on television. He explained that many private schools don't have the same stringent requirements as public schools; that I could begin teaching and work on a certification and a master's later. Within a week, I had a job at a private school that had just received a grant to begin a television program.

I was in! I'd found someone who valued my experience! I found the students also respected my work in the "real world," and within a week on the job, I realized I'd found my new passion. I love everything about teaching—from the energy and enthusiasm of the students to the sense of accomplishment when I watch the student-run broadcasts we produce. After just a month on the job, the principal approached me about teaching full-time the next year. I now teach English, creative writing, and speech along with broadcast journalism.

Then I was approached to take over a course he'd been teaching at the University of Cincinnati, where they had a few adjunct positions for professionals without advanced degrees. I realized that's often an easy "in" for those looking to break into teaching: taking the freshman classes the tenured types think are beneath them. I'm still planning to get my master's degree, but now I have three great jobs that all complement each other—two in teaching and one in television news. I refused to let my age and my lack of credentials, which could be considered other people's strengths, be my weaknesses.

The Arsenal That Improves with Age

Don't let the young-'uns' superpowers depress you. It's not like we more experienced workers don't have our own tricks up our sleeves. A general consensus of top human resources professionals points out that those over forty have the following strengths:

They have extreme job commitment. They take pride in their work, and are not satisfied until they've completed a task to the best of their abilities. Although they will gladly accept a reward for a job well done, they don't expect it, and understand that doing their work to the best of their abilities is standard operating procedure.

They're low-maintenance. They do not require constant praise and feedback. In fact, they like to be left alone to complete a task. While the younger worker will be texting her supervisors constantly to complain, get feedback, fish for compliments, or simply to give an update on the health of her cat who chewed through her DSL cord, the older worker will quietly and confidently solve her own problems and complete her work well before the deadline. The supervisors count on that and, incidentally, will pay more for it.

They're competitive. They were raised to believe that the harder you work, the more you achieve. In school it wasn't just about getting an A, it was about getting a higher grade than anyone else in the class. If someone else is doing better in the workplace, the over-forty worker will try to work harder and faster to keep up and perhaps surpass. The downside of that is that they sometimes succumb to calculation, manipulation, backstabbing, and ruthlessness in order to excel. But they are extremely motivated.

They have outstanding interpersonal skills. They're used to communicating with people face-to-face, and are good at handling the public on a personal level. They are empathetic and try to focus on how the other person feels, rather than being absorbed in how they themselves feel.

They're known for being observant and sensitive. Part of this comes from being engaged in the world around them, rather than growing up with ear pods firmly inserted and wrapped in their own little musical world.

They're loyal. The closer they get to retirement, the more important it becomes to build up their savings and stick with one company that will help do that. They're not likely to leave one employer for another just because the work sounds fun or a friend works there. They're less likely to leave a company high and dry after several months of training.

Don't think for a second that these are old-fashioned virtues that are no longer valued in the workplace. They recently proved to be worth more than $25,000 to one Baby Boomer. Maria was hired to launch and run a website for a major corporation that hired a Gen X'er to launch another website at the same time. She was told not to discuss her salary with the Gen X'er, because she was to be paid substantially more, although they would be doing roughly the same amount of work. Why? Sure, Maria had more experience and connections, but she was also told she was lower-maintenance—that they could trust her to do her work quickly and efficiently without needing a lot of management and oversight. Her superiors told her that they knew their time would be taken up with the Gen X'er constantly contacting them for input and feedback. The Boomer's dedication, independence, and industriousness were worth $25K to them.

Fun Fact

There are approximately 56.7 million U.S. Baby Boomers online, making them the largest group of Internet users in America. They use the Internet more as a tool—as a way to research and get things done—rather than as their preferred source of entertainment and socialization, as younger users do. They prefer e-mail to instant messaging or texting.

So you see, there is absolutely no reason to buy into the hype that younger is always better and more desirable. Madison Avenue may be pushing that message on us, as you can't help but notice from the glossy pages of fashion magazines. By the way, have you noticed how well those magazines are doing lately? With the major loss of ad pages and revenues, they're becoming as anorexic-looking as their models, and many are on the verge of extinction, if they haven't folded already. Behind closed doors, where the vast majority of workers toil away, it's all about performance, not profile. Employers these days simply can't afford to tolerate unproductive habits from any age group. If you learn from and adapt to the strengths of other generations and minimize your own generation's weaknesses, you'll present a powerful package that no employer can resist.

Millionaire Matchmaker Patti Stanger Speaks Out About Generational Work Habits

Say what you will about the bold and brash personal style of Patti Stanger, Bravo's Millionaire Matchmaker, the bottom line is that the woman has a brilliant head for business. I should know. I've been friends with her for almost a decade now, and I helped her write her book *Become Your Own Matchmaker: 8 Easy Steps for Attracting Your Perfect Mate*. I watched her build her company, the Millionaire's Club, from a handful of business cards and a laptop to a multimillion-dollar, international organization with its own television show. And Patti did it all by herself, with her major success coming after she reached the age of forty. She was not the beneficiary of a wealthy husband, a generous trust fund, or deep-pocketed investors, not even particularly good luck. Patti is all about the blood, sweat, and tears that go into a career, and she has poured out more of those in the past ten years than most of us will in a lifetime.

As I write this, Patti is in her late forties, and has not only hired and fired an army of workers but has been a pal and confidante to hundreds of powerful business leaders, both male and female—they make up the majority of her client list. They know she's a pro, and her "tell Momma all about it" demeanor encourages them to confide in her on all sorts of topics, including hiring and firing. They're a good representation of the people who could ultimately be responsible for hiring and firing you.

So, from her own unique perspective (Patti has extremely high standards and expectations) and from the perspective of her successful clients, she shares the following insights on the work habits of the various generations. Remember to see if any of your work habits match up, eliminate the negative ones, and embrace the positive.

"Generation Y starts fires. People over forty put them out. Younger workers grew up in a time of complete media overload. They click on something newer, bigger, better, brighter every five seconds. They have millions of channels, websites, bandwidths, etc., to choose from, so they go toward the one that is the most sensational at the moment. They're constantly socializing electronically, so rumors and scandals spread like crazy. They're all about the drama, and feel the need to share it with everyone—friends, coworkers, the Kinko's guy, whomever. All these habits are very distracting in the workplace.

"On the other hand, workers over forty are more focused on the job at hand, and less distracted by their BlackBerrys. They're more willing to stay late and finish the job, because they're not so anxious to run out and meet their friends at a bar or club. When a crisis arises, the more experienced worker rolls up her sleeves and digs in to solve it, knowing that it won't be fun or pleasant, but that it must be done. The young worker throws her hands in the air, shrieks, 'I can't handle this stress!' and runs out to get a soothing mani and pedi.

"The vast majority of the CEOs I know prefer older, more settled, more experienced assistants. They might try a young hottie patottie for a while, but if the CEO is male, the second his wife sees a sweet young thing at the assistant's desk, trouble starts at home. And if that's not an issue, her competence will be. If she's more into her looks and friends than she is into her job, she'll eventually start affecting his bottom line, and that's when he'll fire her and hire her aunt. All it takes is one 'Wire transfer? What wire transfer?' for him to realize that he needs to hire more on basis of experience and competence than on looks. This is not to say that the woman over forty is not hot. She can be smokin', but her looks will be backed up by her experience. She's the perfect package.

"Unless she doesn't know how to use the Internet. Whether you have your own business or are working for someone else, you are nothing without the Web. My business, my book, my TV show, everything, I repeat, everything, is enhanced a hundred times thanks to the Internet. Ladies, erase the tech advantages younger workers have over you and learn to work the Web!"

Fun Fact

The one thing that unites us all: shopping! It's the first Internet usage that appeals equally to Baby Boomers, Gen Y, and Gen X. It is the one area in which all generations are equally comfortable.

3

Refresh Yourself!

The trick is growing up without growing old.

—*Casey Stengel*

About a year ago I'm sitting there in a private screening room waiting for an independent film to start, and I hear a group of twenty-somethings behind me using words like "hulu," "tweet," and "twitter." I'm thinking, "either they're talking about a Hawaiian bird, or I'm hopelessly out of it." After doing a couple of immediate Google searches on my Dare (which was the closest thing Verizon had to an iPhone at the time. What? I had a two-year contract I couldn't break!), I discovered that the answer was, "I'm hopelessly out of it." And here I was priding myself on being technologically cutting-edge. I should have known I'd get in trouble eavesdropping on a conversation between Gen Y'ers. That's what I get.

Trying to keep up with the latest in tech, entertainment, pop culture, and fashion can make you crazy, but if you're going to compete in today's youth-obsessed job market, you might as well at least take a stab at it. You don't want to be sitting in an interview with a twenty-eight-year-old and get blindsided with a term that leaves you completely clueless and shows that you're not current. You also don't want your new coworkers to avoid conversation with you because they have to define every other word they use.

The greatest thing about keeping up, however, is how it makes you *feel*. Current, hip, chic, savvy, and cool are all adjectives that immediately come to mind. When you're riding in an elevator with a bunch of girls who look like they just graduated college and one of them squeals, "Oh my God! I love your sweater! Barney's?" you know you've arrived. It doesn't matter if you got your sweater at Target, what does matter is that they believe you're cool and successful enough to shop at Barney's.

So let's see how far you have to go to get there. Here's a quiz that will let you know just . . .

How Hip Are You?

1. Hulu is:
   A: A designer drug
   B: A hip-hop dance
   C: A TV- and film-viewing website
   D: A greeting

2. Seven for All Mankind is:
   A: A worldwide charity founded by Leonardo DiCaprio
   B: A jeans manufacturer
   C: A Kabbalah-based religion
   D: A particularly nasty computer virus

3. When you "wiki" something, you:
   A: Smoke it
   B: Dispose of it
   C: Suck it through a straw
   D: Look it up on a site online

4. Who is Lloyd?
   A: Ari's assistant on *Entourage*
   B: The Google mascot
   C: The creepy janitor on *Gossip Girls*
   D: Joe Biden's notorious brother-in-law

5. These days, when you "hook up" you:
   A: Meet casually, as in for lunch or drinks
   B: Have sex
   C: Do a favor for someone
   D: Take advantage of something

6. Will.i.am is:

    A: A rapper, singer, and songwriter

    B: A legal document service

    C: A brand of designer dog food

    D: A character in the book *Green Eggs and Ham*, which is cur-
    rently being made into a movie

7. What is a carbon footprint?

    A: What's left in the bong after you smoke

    B: A measure of your impact on the environment

    C: Marks left after you've stepped in dog poo

    D: Dinosaur tracks

8. What is DS?

    A: Twitter shorthand for "Dude sucks!"

    B: A discreet abbreviation for "downsize"

    C: A raised platform in a banquet hall where speakers and guests
    of honor sit

    D: A handheld video game console from Nintendo

9. TMZ stands for:

    A: Thirty Mile Zone

    B: Too Much Zing

    C: The Malicious Zap

    D: Tom Marshall's Zoo

10. According to employers and plastic surgeons, which of the follow-
    ing cosmetic procedures is most likely to enhance your hireability?

    A: Botox

    B: Rhinoplasty(nose job)

    C: Tattoo removal

    D: Breast enhancement

11. Huffpo is:

    A: A nickname for a bad-girl society heirness

    B: A children's TV show that helped form Gen Y values

C: Slang for a burned-out drug addict

D: An abbreviation for a popular news and political blog

12. Which of the following is *not* a social networking site?

A: MySpace

B: Bebo

C: Grokster

D: Facebook

13. An Avatar is:

A: Your online alter ego

B: A pterodactyl-type comic book creature from the future

C: A military rank in a popular community computer game

D: A vial used for mixing perfume

14. Who is Judd Apatow?

A: One of the founders of Google

B: A comedy writer/director/producer

C: A former member of the Brat Pack who currently stars in a TV legal drama

D: Kate Winslet's first husband, with whom she has a son

15. Kindle is:

A: The hottest new Hermès designer bag

B: The most popular name for girls in 2009

C: A social networking site

D: A digital book reading device

16. The two main characters in the Twilight series are:

A: Sookie and Bill

B: Elizabeth and Barnabus

C: Bella and Edward

D: Cassandra and Theodore

17. What superpower does Peter Petrelli (from *Heroes*) have?

    A: Reading minds

    B: Super speed

    C: Flying

    D: Absorbing others' powers

18. Which is not a popular band?

    A: Plain White Tees

    B: Cute Is What We Aim For

    C: Blue Night

    D: The Ting Tings

19. Jennifer Aniston and Jessica Simpson have this man in common:

    A: John Mayer

    B: Tony Romo

    C: Brad Pitt

    D: Nick Lachey

20. Who is Kara DioGuardi?

    A: A popular Food Network chef know for cooking in lingerie

    B: That first designer to start her own successful line after winning *Project Runway*

    C: A very outspoken congresswoman from Delaware who wears designer labels

    D: The newest *American Idol* judge

21. Which one is *not* an energy drink?

    A: Pimp Juice

    B: Monster

    C: JitSu

    D: Hi Octane

22. SXSW is:

    A: A music, film, and interactive conference and festival

    B: An adult website that focuses on sex and swingers

C: A cable TV show that involves teams searching for buried treasure

D: Nicolas Cage's latest Asian apocalyptic film

23. If you "face" someone, you:

A: Embarrass them

B: Outdo them

C: Look them in the eye straight on

D: Contact them via Facebook

24. Housewives from which geographical area have not had a Bravo reality show produced about them?

A: Orange County

B: Atlanta

C: New York

D: Malibu

25. Gawker is:

A: A Web search engine

B: A daily gossip and news blog

C: Someone who tries to read other people's text messages

D: A pop culture addict

Answers:

1. C: A TV- and film-viewing website
2. B: A jeans manufacturer
3. D: Look it up on a site online
4. A: Ari's assistant on *Entourage*
5. B: Have sex
6. A: A rapper, singer, and songwriter
7. B: A measure of your impact on the environment
8. D: A handheld video game console from Nintendo
9. A: Thirty Mile Zone
10. C: Tattoo removal
11. D: An abbreviation for a popular news and political blog
12. C: Grokster

13. A: Your online alter ego
14. B: A comedy writer/director/producer
15. D: A digital book reading device
16. C: Bella and Edward
17. D: Absorbing others' powers
18. C: Blue Night
19. A: John Mayer
20. D: The newest *American Idol* judge
21. D: Hi Octane
22. A: A music, film, and interactive conference and festival
23. D: Contact them via Facebook
24. D: Malibu
25. B: A daily gossip and news blog

21–25: You are ageless, hipper than hip, could start your own pop culture blog, could judge a beauty pageant, and should be hosting your own talk show. You probably get carded every time you go into a bar, and twentysomething members of the opposite sex often hit on you. If you have teenagers, you are more popular with their friends than they are.

16–20: Congrats! You'll understand most conversations going on around you and you won't embarrass your kids. Just to be sure, though, scan the weekly entertainment magazines at the checkout counter, and pay attention to the culture, entertainment, and style sections of a newspaper, newsmagazine, or news website.

11–15: You're not completely out of it, but you need to brush up on current culture if you don't want to be referred to as an "old fart." Even watching Oprah and/or *The View* would help, but scanning TMZ.com or some other pop culture site regularly and reading *People* every now and then will really help, along with going through the most recent edition of *InStyle*. If that makes you shudder, the least you can do is listen to NPR regularly. You'd be surprised how hip they are.

1–10: If you didn't even get half of these right, you have a lot of catching up to do and desperately need a daily infusion of hipness from several different sources. NPR is a must, but also try tuning into the daily info-tainment shows like *Access Hollywood* and *Extra!*, surfing the Internet, reading weekly entertainment magazines, and eavesdropping on the conversations of the young people around you; you can always go home and Google any words or references you don't understand.

Instant Hip

I've cooked up my own little crash course in current culture. If you try at least ten of the following suggestions, not only will you be better connected with the world around you, but you'll be able to commiserate with and understand people several decades younger than you are, and your kids will look at you with renewed respect. In addition, you'll feel invigorated and refreshed, with the confidence to run with the coolest of them. You don't have to make a habit out of any of these things if they don't suit you, but just knowing you can and have done them gives you a tremendous youth infusion.

20 Ways to Raise Your Hip Quotient

1. Get TiVo or the digital recording device most accessible to you, and learn how to use it. More than 29 million Baby Boomers are doing this already—you don't want to be left behind! Author Jackie Collins once told me she has eight television sets recording some show or other constantly, because she's a pop culture addict and just can't get enough. Oh, and she's reported to be in her seventies and still writes books that sell millions of copies.

2. Drink a Red Bull, and if you really want to get a dose of what they're swilling in clubs these days, order a cocktail of Red Bull and vodka. Don't even *think* about driving home afterward, and make sure you drink it at least six hours before going to bed, or you'll never get to sleep. Personally, I find the taste and feeling dreadful, but I now under-stand how so many people around me are buzzing all night.

3. Read *Twilight*, or any of the books in the series by Stephenie Meyer.

4. Play *Guitar Hero*, *Grand Theft Auto*, *Halo*, or any other current video game. If there isn't a kid in your neighborhood that has it, go to your nearest big-box electronics store and check out the demonstrations they have set up. By the way, this isn't as outlandish as it may sound—it's estimated that more than seven million people over fifty own gaming devices, even though they don't have kids. I'm among them. Wii can help keep you fit and is a great entertainment station at parties.

5. Go jeans shopping at the hippest store in town. You don't have to buy anything—you don't even have to try on anything. You can say that you're shopping for your niece, and talk to the salesperson to get an idea of what's big in denim. (Don't go with the obvious pun here.)

6. Send a text message to someone. Ask for a reply, read it, and respond. Or if that's too easy for you, start following someone on Twitter.

7. Commit to scanning at least one current culture or news blog daily. Depending on your interests, you might want to try: Huffington Post.com, wowowow.com, wsj.com. nytimes.com, thedailybeast.com, dailyfill.com, gawker.com, jezebel.com, or yahoo.com.

8. Subscribe to at least one online newsletter. Websites for most major newspapers have them—this is how I read the *New York Times* without subscribing, although free services like these could end at any moment. Find the top website for your own particular field or profession. Since I'm involved with media, I subscribe to several, but I particularly like Cynopsis.com and MediaBistro.com, both of which list professional opportunities on a daily basis, in addition to keeping me up on the latest news in my field. SmartBrief.com covers a number of different professions, and offers daily newsletters keeping you up on the latest in advertising, social media, broadcasting, etc. I subscribe to four of their newsletters.

9. Listen to the best-selling songs on iTunes, purchase one, and learn how to download it so you can play it whenever you want. It should cost only around a dollar. Any computer that's been updated in the past five years should be capable of this. If your computer hasn't been updated in the past five years, put that at the top of your list.

10. Take a picture of something fun on your cell phone and send it to someone. Again, if you've purchased a decent cell phone in the past five years, it should have this capability. Sending the photo might be an additional, minimal cost.

11. Start a Facebook page for yourself. Look me up under Lisa Johnson Mandell, author, send me a message, and I'll be your first friend. To get started, search for friends from school, then expand to former business associates, and move on to people who you'd like to be connected with professionally. Avoid contacting your kids or their friends. You will embarrass them. More on this in chapter 7.

12. Sign up for a fitness boot camp. They're being offered in just about every town now, and they combine so many different kinds of exercise you're bound to enjoy some part of it.

13. Test-drive a hybrid. Even if a new car is not in your budget in the near future, try driving one to see what all the buzz is about. You might end up making it your first purchase after you get your new job.

14. Google yourself. If there's not much out there about you, you'll find fascinating info about people who have your same name. Maybe you'll want to start a club with them. Now Google the people closest to you. Hey, you can even Google me, just for the fun of it. Last I checked you would be able to see my wedding photos.

15. Go to YouTube.com and watch the ten most viewed videos. I guarantee you will get a good laugh out of them, and you might even find something you want to embed on your own blog site (more on that in chapter 6).

16. Watch an episode of your favorite TV show online. You can probably find it on its network website or on hulu.com. New research shows that people in the eighteen- to thirty-four-year-old age group prefer this to watching TiVo or any other digital recording system.

17. Get some sleep! While you're sleeping, your body defuses stress, repairs and grows cells—even burns fat! Why deprive yourself of something so effortless, beneficial, and just plain wonderful? Make a real effort to get at least eight hours per night, even if you have to rearrange your schedule and make some serious sacrifices. Ever wish you had the same energy you had when you were a teenager or in college? Ever notice how late students sleep in? One of the reasons younger people seem to have so much more energy is that they get so much more sleep.

18. Adopt a pet. If you already have one, adopt another. Living creatures inspire childlike wonder, even if it's just a goldfish. Watching, interacting with, and caring for your pet can relax you and relieve everyday stress, which helps you feel rejuvenated and refreshed. Warning: Make sure you don't gush over your pet incessantly whenever you chat with others, and don't get too many cats.

19. Make a platonic date with a twentysomething. Offer to buy her lunch in exchange for going through your closet and helping you get rid of everything that's hopelessly dated. Or simply chat while you get manicures and pedicures. Listen to her!

20. Paint your toenails dark purple, blue, or black. Show them off for at least a day, wearing sandals. Warning: Do not do this on the day of a job interview.

If you have children, nieces, nephews, or neighbors in their late teens or early twenties, spending some dedicated time with them is the perfect place to start getting caught up. Take them shopping, take them to lunch, or simply hang out and watch them surf the Net while they're listening to their favorite music. Have you ever seen a kid online who's not listening to his or her favorite music? Try actually listening to them and pay close attention to their vocabulary. If you're like me, you'll be temporarily distracted by their grammatical errors and will tune out as you mentally correct them. But stay focused! Also, pay close attention to what they're doing online, how they communicate, what sites they spend the most time with, viewing, downloading, shopping, getting news, etc. You can always offer to pay them a decent hourly wage to get you and your computer all caught up.

If you don't have access to any young people, call on a service like Geek Squad, FastTeks.com, GeeksOnCall.com, or MakeItWork.com to at least update your computer. Personally, I've only used the Geek Squad and can recommend them—they'll help you with all sorts of electronic gadgets, like your cell phone, your digital recording device, your BlackBerry, just about anything technological that stumps you, in addition to your computer. I've also heard great things about MakeIt Work.com.

ADVICE FROM A DESPERATE HOUSEWIFE

I don't think there's anyone out there over forty who seems fresher, hipper, or more beautiful than actress Teri Hatcher, who has staged what could be considered a number of career comebacks, taking the occasional TV or film role in between hit series like *Lois & Clark: The New Adventures of Superman* and *Desperate Housewives*. When speaking to her about her lead voice role in *Coraline*, the first stop-motion animated 3-D movie ever (how hip and cutting-edge is *that*?), she told me a little bit about what she does to feel like she's on top of her game: The secret lies in not trying too hard; not trying to be superwoman, knowing and being all things at all times. She says the pressure will really take its toll on you if you try to be the fabulous wife and mother with the amazing career all in the same moment. "You have to acknowledge and accept the fact that you can't have or be everything all at the same time," she says. Imposing that kind of pressure on yourself can make you old, stressed out, overloaded, and ungrateful for all the things you *do* have at that moment. She also notes that you need to communicate those feelings to the people around you. "I think we run around trying to be perfect all the time and we keep our feelings about it inside, rather than just sitting down in a calm way and saying, 'Some days I'm able to go to work and go to the soccer game and make the dinner but today we have to order pizza.' Instead of constantly pushing ourselves, we need to accept and even teach our kids about our own limitations."

So much is expected of women in particular these days, and nothing seems to make us seem old and bitter faster than misplaced stress. Even those of us without children feel the pressure to look, feel, and act perfect at all times, both on the job and off. If relieving that pressure works for Teri Hatcher, who is even more gorgeous and sparkling in person than she is onscreen, we would all be well advised to try it.

Give Yourself Some Lee-Way

Although few of us have the resources to look lovely and fit and care for our children the way a celebrity like Teri Hatcher does, her advice works for those of us in the trenches as well. Just ask Lee Rappaport, a beautiful and extremely energetic woman in her mid-fifties. Lee has always been ahead of the curve professionally; she was successfully buying and selling on eBay back in 1998, when most people were just starting to use e-mail. She didn't find her true professional passion, however, until she reached her early fifties, when she became a local childcare coordinator with Cultural Care Au Pair. She has been careful to explain to her family all along the way that she needs to take time to grow and accomplish things on her own, so that she can be better equipped to help them reach their full potential. As a result, at an age when some people are looking longingly toward retirement, Lee has the energy and spirit to utilize the latest technology and social networking devices to make the most of her relatively new career.

"Twitter, Facebook, LinkedIn—I use them to stay connected with the families and the au pairs, not to mention prospective clients and the friends who return to their respective countries," she says. Lee helps orchestrate a cultural exchange program in which qualified, international childcare workers (au pairs) are placed in homes in the United States. She also organizes cultural and social events for the au pairs, even taking them into her home when the circumstances warrant it. "This job gives me so many opportunities to learn so much about other people and cultures. You never stop growing with this position," she says.

Thirty years ago, when people reached their mid-fifties, they were starting to gear down, to wind things up, professionally speaking. But those times have changed. Lee sees it as an invigorating challenge and a blessing that technology, among other things, enables us to go full speed ahead for as long as we feel like it. "I'm able to do my job better, with much more confidence now than I ever could have had twenty years ago," she enthuses. "I thought I was hot stuff back then. I'm *really* hot stuff now!"

Lose Ten Years Instantly—Free!

I know I sound like a bad radio ad, but most experts agree that one of the most effective rejuvenating methods available is...drumroll, please...exercise! Sure, you've heard it all before, but energy is a "use it or lose it" commodity. If you want more, you have to expend more. It's just that simple. Estimates of how much exercise you need are varied, but many suggest at least thirty minutes of heart-pumping activity five times a week, or fifty minutes three times a week, whichever you prefer. If it's any help, know that most American kids don't even get that much exercise, so if you do, you'll be way ahead of them.

Exercise doesn't have to be sweaty, gross, and painful. Taking a quick walk outside is not only a great way to work out, but a fabulous way to socialize, network, and meet your neighbors. If you use an iPod or radio, you can listen to podcasts, audiobooks, NPR, or the latest music. Find some form of exercise that really works for you, that you really enjoy and even look forward to. I'm on what I like to call the Netflix Diet. It involves about forty minutes a day on the treadmill or elliptical machine while I watch a DVD I've rented. I won't allow myself to watch that particular DVD unless I'm working out. The better the movie, the more I work out. And if it has a lively soundtrack that really moves me, I'm like the Tasmanian Devil. Between that and my daily dog walks with my golden doodle, KC, I'm sufficiently fit and I know most of my neighbors.

Notice that I'm suggesting exercise as a way to *feel* better, but of course the great by-product is that it will make you *look* better as well. You'll stand up straighter, your muscles will be tighter, and you'll have a confident, endorphin-infused glow. I always try to get in a workout a couple hours before any important appointment or interview. I'm certainly not going to tell you to exercise so you can get down to any ideal size. There isn't one. The ideal size for you is the one at which you feel the most energetic and confident.

The Key to Irresistibility at Any Age

Even if you're the fittest, hippest person in the room, know everything "the kids" know, and do everything "the kids" do, if you're missing one basic attribute, you'll look and feel far older than you actually are, and you'll be passed up for that dream job every time. That one quality is— you guessed it—a positive attitude. Nothing sucks the air out of a room faster than a negative attitude, and nothing revitalizes people quicker than confident, supportive optimism.

Think about it. We all have that one friend or family member who seems to walk around under a cloud. It's the Benjamin Button who seems to be born eighty-five and cranky. You avoid them at all costs, because you know you're going to feel angry, depressed, or dissatisfied after seeing them. They're the people who always find the one weed in your brilliantly blooming flowerbed, the one gray hair on your otherwise ebony head. Employers don't want to hire these people because they bring their coworkers down and productivity drops, not to mention the fact that they're boring and they complain about everything. On the other hand, the person who exudes positive energy is always a welcome (and rare) addition.

If you're having trouble mustering positive energy—and to be sure, when times are tough and you're out of work, it's not easy to flick on that switch—it can help tremendously to develop an attitude of gratitude. As clichéd as this may sound, try to count your blessings and focus on all the things you do have, rather than the things you don't have. Take mental inventory of all your talents and attributes, rather than dwelling on the things you're not and wish you were. Think about everything you've accomplished up to this point in your life, instead of observing others your own age who seem to have achieved so much more. Try not to be the proverbial "hater."

Recently my husband and I were on our way to the Critics Choice Awards, decked out in glamorous black tie and eager to enjoy one of the best evenings of the year. A call came in over the Bluetooth device in my car and my husband automatically clicked the answer button on the steering wheel, without looking at the screen that would tell him who was calling. It was a friend of ours, a C-list celebrity whose name you would probably recognize. The guy was at the top of his game: easily clearing seven figures that year, had just had his own TV show renewed for another season, and the book he'd just released was selling like crazy. Yet all he could do was complain about the fact that his publicist couldn't get him on *Oprah*. He was spewing verbal venom and using some of the worst language I'd ever heard. My husband, being far more assertive than I am, said, "Hey, buddy—you sound like a grumpy old man! Why do you want to ruin the air in our car with all that toxicity? Most people never achieve a tenth of what you've done, and all you can do is complain about some minor wrinkle in your otherwise perfect life. Why don't you just hang up now and think about all the amazing things that have come your way. We'll catch you later." I wanted to kiss my hubby right then and there, in the middle of the 405.

Call it karma, the secret, prayer, what goes around comes around, whatever, I'm a firm believer that what you put out there comes back to you. If you spend your time and energy in positive endeavors, of course you'll make some headway in that direction. Treat people nicely and respectfully, and they'll treat you the same way. The reverse is also true. Spend enough time dwelling on the negative, and it can't help but show up more often in your life—not only are you willing it to happen, but you'll notice the minor disturbances more. If you think of yourself as unlucky, untalented, ungifted, that's exactly how you'll come across.

No matter how bad things seem, try to remember they could always be worse. Even if you've been searching for a job for six months and haven't had any decent prospects yet, if you're not starving or dying and you have a roof over your head, you're actually doing better than a good portion of the world population. So in the major scope of things, your complaints are minor. And by the way, no one wants to hear you gripe—about anything. Negativity is just a bore. Do you want to be known as a buzz kill?

On a professional level, no interviewer wants to hear a litany of complaints about your former job or employer, or about how difficult your current situation is and how desperately you need this job. They want to hire someone who will uplift and energize clients and staff, not someone who is going to bring everyone down and foment dissatisfaction. You need to be the one who brings light into a room, not the one who causes darkness. Granted, it's important to be able to recognize problems and know how to solve them, but instead of crying that "this can ruin everything!" you need to declare that "we can fix this and make it better."

A fresh, hip, positive attitude can go a long way toward getting you the job you want, but you're also going to have to look the part of the successful, competent, current colleague. Next up: How to revitalize your appearance and dress to impress.

4

Look the Part

When it comes to staying young, a mind-lift beats a face-lift any day.

—*Marty Bucella*

Now that you're feeling intellectually and culturally fresh and hip, it's time to start looking the part. After all, there are still plenty of shallow employers out there who have no interest in finding out about what's on the inside if they can't see some hint of interest on the outside. So if you're feeling fresh and hip, why not radiate it? It's not half as difficult, or expensive, as you might imagine.

The first and easiest place to start is only a few steps away—in your closet. If you haven't worked full-time for a while, if you're just entering the workforce, if you're changing careers, or if you've been with the same company for a very long time, chances are your wardrobe could use some updating. Even if the salesclerk insisted that navy blue suit was a "timeless classic that would never go out of style" when you bought it ten years ago before the kids came along, I can pretty much guarantee you it's not going to work for you in today's business environment.

But before you purge everything, know that you might be able to make some of your old pieces new by combining them in a fresher way—everyone has a long-sleeved white blouse, for example. Instead of tucking it in, you can leave it untucked, and perhaps belted—that's an immediate wardrobe freshener. That navy jacket that went with the suit might look fine now with jeans and a T-shirt or a bright-colored blouse, as would a Chanel-type jacket. And high-waisted, pleated pants are actually back in fashion now—you can wear them with your crisp white shirt and a scarf at your neck and look very Katharine Hepburn, which has always been in style.

I updated my own wardrobe the hard, humiliating way. When my husband convinced me I needed to have some young, vibrant photos taken, I was in a complete quandary about what to wear to the photo session. I needed three distinct looks, one casual, one professional, and one somewhere in between, and I was drawn to my old standards that had always served me well—the classic gray skirted suit, the black turtleneck, perhaps a pretty sweater and wool pants. Just to be on the safe side, however, I invited a twenty-six-year-old media-savvy girlfriend over to help me decide. As she pawed through my closet, I heard her snicker and sniff every now and then. "What's the matter?" I asked. "Is it that bad?"

"Lisa," she started, "no offense, but when was the last time you wore this fuchsia blazer with the massive shoulder pads? You need to get rid of it before you're ever tempted to wear it again. And these tight knit miniskirts? You've got great legs, but no one over forty should be caught dead in these things. Oh, and unless you're wearing a long tank under some of these shorter tops, they have to go as well. Even if your stomach is hard as a rock and flat as a board, no one wants to see middle-aged middle. I'm just sayin'…"

Ulp! I immediately ripped all the offending garments off their hangers and put them in the Goodwill bag. Once my closet had considerably more space, we were able to find three outfits to wear to my photo shoot: straight-legged jeans, high-heeled black boots, and a studded rock 'n' roll T-shirt with an unintelligible logo on it; a classic slate blue BCBG wrap dress with fawn-colored high-heeled slingbacks; and she allowed me to wear the classic black turtleneck, but I was to pair it with a leopard-print pencil skirt and black stilettos.

Turns out my girlfriend's judgment was spot-on—not only did the photos help me get a number of job offers, but whenever a news source does a piece on me and they run those pictures, I get dozens of queries about where I got my clothes. (You'll note one of those photos is featured prominently on the cover of this book.) You already know my dirty little secret about that outfit: The rock 'n' roll T-shirt was a hand-me-down from my seventy-two-year-old mother. There's nothing wrong with a septuagenarian who likes to wear Skinny Minnie.

For some of the best, rejuvenating fashion advice available, I've called upon international style expert Charla Krupp, author of *How Not to Look Old*, to give you a few pointers on updating your own wardrobe. I first met Charla when we did a segment together on "Botox for Your Résumé" for the CBS *Early Show*. She very kindly and tactfully stopped me before I went on camera and reaccessorized me, lending me a pair of her own earrings! That way, when we were being interviewed she could say I was the perfect, ageless example of a hip professional. Charla's book, by the way, goes on beyond clothing and gives suggestions for hair, makeup, skin care, and more, and I highly recommend it. What follows are Charla's lists of a Dozen Items to Toss, and a Dozen Must-Haves, all for the chic professional.

12 Items You Need to Throw Away Now

1. A handbag with a photo of your children or dogs on it
2. Scrunchies and banana clips for the hair
3. Jewel-colored blazers with big shoulder pads
4. Nude panty hose
5. Orthopedic-looking rubber-sole shoes
6. Granny glasses
7. Chains for your glasses
8. Down parkas that hit mid-calf or below
9. Overalls
10. T-shirts with not-so-funny sayings such as "I'm with stupid"
11. Holiday sweaters
12. Fanny packs

12 Must-Haves for Every Hip Professional Woman

1. A black pencil skirt
2. A pair of high heels that you can actually walk in
3. An of-the-moment, classy handbag
4. A high-waisted "shapewear" foundation garment, like bike shorts
5. Black opaque tights
6. Perfect-fit, boot-cut dark denim jeans
7. A cool, important-looking watch

8. The right size bra that lifts you up
9. A pair of to-the-knee, tight-fit brown or black heeled boots
10. A long statement necklace
11. Diamond studs—real or faux
12. The perfect crisp white cotton long-sleeved blouse

The Great Stocking Debate

I know that some of you did a double take when you read that you should get rid of your nude panty hose. Your mother wore them, your grandmother wore them, you've been wearing them for dress-up occasions since you were twelve, and you feel naked without them. I hate to tell you this, ladies, but they are completely, 100 percent obsolete. Nothing says old, frumpy, and out of it faster than flesh-colored stockings. I'm aware that there are some work environments that require a woman's legs to be covered, as in certain courts and religious organizations, so if you must wear stockings, the absolute sheerest possible are best, so that they're almost invisible, and if you get a run no one will notice. Colored opaque tights also work well. I haven't bought a pair of panty hose for at least eight years.

Some of you in the Midwest will be especially resistant to this, thinking maybe New Yorkers or Californians can get away with bare legs, but not respectable women in the heartland. Again, try to take your cue from talk show hosts and news anchors—most of them wouldn't be caught dead in panty hose anymore. Do you recall the flap several years ago about Katie Couric not wearing panty hose? If you need a little extra support, shapewear is fabulous for control of the tummy and thighs, but trust me, control-top panty hose are not going to present you in your best, freshest light. If you don't like the way your legs look without stockings, cover them up with a longer skirt, boots, opaque tights, or well-fitting pants. Yes, there are some people who can still get away with nonsheer panty hose. My seventy-three-year-old mother wears them to church and looks great. But she retired a while back after teaching first grade for about forty years. So if you want to dress like a seventy-three-year-old retired schoolteacher on her way to Sunday school, wear panty hose.

If you're thinking about purchasing a few more new pieces for your professional wardrobe, you'll of course want to select styles that will last beyond the interviews and into the job, and will work for you for a decent amount of time. How do you know what to wear in today's ever-changing workplace? Unless your job requires a lab coat, scrubs, or a uniform, there are basically three types of environments or cultures that you're likely to encounter in the professional working world: **business casual, creative chic, and executive/corporate.**

Business Casual

In fields such as education, engineering, service, Internet, construction, medicine, insurance, high tech, and most retail (unless it's high fashion), you'll be wearing a business casual look, which will also serve you well on a Casual Friday in a corporate environment.

Cardigans, sweaters, light jackets or blazers, full, comfy knit skirts that don't constrict, blouses, and dressy T-shirts (especially worn layered) are all appropriate. Comfort and practicality are very important in these fields—a teacher, for example, can't be worrying about dry cleaning her favorite skirt every time she wears it. But that doesn't mean she should take the liberty of wearing baggy, faded cotton pants every day. Also, no matter what the men are wearing, unless you're under thirty and working for a dot-com, a T-shirt, jeans, and tennies are a little too casual, but you probably can get away with drawstring pants, cargoes, and capris. Shorts, unless they're knee-length and dressy, are never an option. Sweatsuits are also no-no's at work, unless you're a coach or personal trainer. Blouses and sweaters are always preferable to casual T-shirts and sweatshirts.

Those over forty should probably not wear tank tops, revealing halters, or anything strappy, even if there's intense heat in your workplace and you've got killer definition in your upper arms. Cap sleeves are fine. People who wear business casual often succumb to the khaki drabs, wearing a lot of beiges, grays, creams, and tans, accented with black or white, because they're really easy to pull together and don't show stains as much. Don't give in to this urge! Adding a little color to your ensemble, no matter how casual, is always a good idea—the right red accents can add pop to any outfit, and a color that makes your eyes sparkle will add freshness, as well as help you stand out from all those wearing khaki, black, or beige. But don't go too extreme with the color. Big prints and extremely bright colors are difficult for anyone to look good in but the very tall—you want to look fresh and hip, not loud and obnoxious.

Creative Chic

If you're going to be working in a field where a distinctive public impression is important, such as public relations, marketing, entertainment, advertising, broadcast journalism, interior design, publishing, special events planning, even corporate support positions where your personal presentation is a reflection on your employer, you'll want to dress for work with a little more style and sophistication. Think talk show hosts, like Oprah, Tyra Banks, Kelly Ripa, the women on *The View*, and news anchors like Katie Couric, Maria Bartiromo, and Maggie Rodriguez. You want to express yourself with color and style, but not err on the side of the clownish or outlandish. Note their use of a single, stunning accessory, like a necklace or scarf, to really make their outfits pop. Grab the latest issue of an age-appropriate magazine (I like *More*) to get an idea of what women in similar fields are wearing and what's being advertised as chic professional wear.

Good fabric and good fit are especially important. Fabrics no longer need to be all natural—there are some stunning blends that drape well and feel like a cloud—but avoid synthetics that pill or snag, or that look too stiff or stretchy. When it comes to fit, baggy often looks sloppy or airy fairy, and tight can appear cheap. Check for wrinkles in odd places (like the crotch) when you're in the dressing room, and unless you plan to have it professionally altered, don't take it home, even if it's on sale for 75 percent off. Never, I repeat, *never*, buy anything thinking that it will look perfect as soon as you drop those lingering five pounds. That pair of pants will sit in the back of your closet forever.

To be specific, a rich-colored silk blouse that's a high contrast with a knee-length pencil skirt, jacket, long necklace, and high heels will definitely make a positive impression, as would a wrap dress that's not too low-cut—wear a cami underneath if it gaps or shows too much cleavage. A little cleavage exposure is fine, but it is possible to display too much of a good thing—you want your colleagues to focus on your work and your ideas, not on your chest. Sleek, not bulky, turtlenecks are good, with a sweater or jacket and tailored pants. Bulky, either on top or bottom, looks mannish and usually too casual. Ruffles can also be a problem—too many during the day can look immature and unprofessional. A ruffle at your neck, around your sleeves, or something subtle around the bottom of your skirt can work, however.

Executive/Corporate

If you're in finance, accounting, law, banking, upper-level management, or in an executive position, a good "power suit" is essential. But don't even think about a skirted version of your father's dull navy, black, or charcoal suit with an ecru shirt. In that outfit you'll look like a boring drone with little or no imagination, and you'll make virtually no impression on anyone. Not that there's anything wrong with suits of those classic colors, but it's important to add a little spark and dazzle to your outfit. How about a red silk blouse? Red is a power color, you know. Button-down shirts are acceptable, but stay away from boring white, cream, or light blue, or anything that would be a staple in a man's wardrobe.

If you want to make a lasting impression, try sparking up your boring classics with a dazzling scarf or statement necklace, as Candice Bergen and Meryl Streep often do when playing professionals and as Hillary Clinton does at almost all times—by the way, these accessories also camouflage crepey, wrinkling, or sagging necks. A classic suit no longer need entail a plain, hip-length jacket and straight, knee-length skirt. Why not try a pencil skirt with a cropped jacket or one belted at the waist, as Julia Roberts wore in the film *Duplicity*? That's a flattering look on almost all body types. Interesting detailing on the lapels, seams, pockets, and hems also adds a chic touch. High-waisted or skinny-legged pants with a shorter-length matching jacket can also combine in a perfectly appropriate statement suit. Coat-length jackets that are even with the bottom of your skirt also make a positive statement, as do matching dress and jacket ensembles.

Interesting, flattering, expensive-*looking* shoes are also musts for the successful executive. Get rid of all those conservative, plain-colored pumps with one- or two-inch chunky heels. Kitten heels are fine, but those practical pumps your mother used to wear with panty hose are out of the question. Also, stay away from any shoe with a strap that resembles a Mary Jane, even if it has high heels—they're too little-girlish and not authoritative enough. Sophisticated flats are fine, but ballet flats don't exude professional power either. You can certainly wear high heels in colors—they don't have to be basic black or brown anymore. Just make sure you can easily walk in them all day.

PROFESSIONAL ADVICE

WALK STRAIGHT TO THE TOP

If you really want a little confident edge with just a touch of sexy intimidation, get yourself a good pair of power heels. Believe me, you'll feel like you're walking on top of the world—just let any man, in his grubby little flat shoes, try to stop you! High heels can put you at eye level with your professional superiors, and eliminate the intimidation of being looked down upon. I wear them to all my important meetings, and call me superstitious, but I always have good luck in them. Maybe it's just because they make me feel like I'm at the top of my game, but I almost always get what I want when I wear them.

If you still have doubts about what's appropriate to wear in your professional setting, you can always talk to a trained style consultant. Some major department stores have them, although ambitious salespeople often claim the title without being qualified. I personally have a lot of confidence in Carlisle Collection representatives. They sell elegant clothing all over the country at in-home trunk shows, and they're often hired by major corporations to help give their female executives a fresh, hip, yet appropriate look. I contacted several Carlisle reps from various parts of the country for universal, professional business dressing tips. (See the resource guide for a Carlisle representative near you.) Here's what they advise:

1. Look like a woman, but don't emphasize your sexy side. This means avoid any tops that are low-cut, too tight, or too sheer. Watch your skirt length and remember that when you sit down it goes up another two inches (slits also rise). Also avoid super-high stilettos that affect the way you walk.

2. Always choose the skirt or dress length that is best for your leg, regardless of what you see strutting down the runways.

3. In grooming, avoid long nails that look like they would impede doing work and hairstyles that partially cover your eyes.

4. Accessories are a must for both traditional business and business casual dressing. Express your individual style with your choices; however, belt loops require a belt and pierced ears must always sport earrings.

5. Watch accessories that detract from people paying attention to what you have to say. Swaying, dangling earrings focus attention on your ears versus your eyes and mouth.

6. To look your trimmest and most sophisticated, try dressing in a "Column of Color," for example, a black top and bottom paired with a jacket of a different color value. This can be a bright or muted color, just so you have a solid column of color right up the middle.

7. Remember that business casual is not the same as weekend casual—sweats, jeans, flip-flops, halter tops, strapless sundresses, and such are not appropriate in most business environments.

8. When in doubt, look to a female superior for an example. It's a good idea, whether you're male or female, not to consistently out-dress those directly above you who could be responsible for your promotions.

9. Focus on quality, not quantity. It's better to own a few fine pieces than many average pieces. Put well-cut pieces in your closet that relate to each other, that have a now-and-later quality to them, that combine to meet your different lifestyle needs, and that bridge seasons and time zones.

10. Your weight, whatever it is, is no excuse to put off organizing a wardrobe that supports your professional image. In the business world, you need to project confidence, credibility, and authority. *All the time.*

11. Remember, fit and size are rarely the same thing. Start with the right size. Then have a good seamstress do the fit. This gives the "couture" touch to your wardrobe.

12. If you want your high-quality clothes to last, spring for a professional steamer. It will save you the expense of dry cleaning, which also puts extra wear and tear on clothes, as does ironing with a hand iron.

Lisa's ADVICE

IT'S IN THE BAG

If you're going to make an investment in one good professional piece, make it a great handbag. This will serve you well during the interview process, and on into your workday once you land that job. It doesn't necessarily have to be a thousand-dollar designer bag. Companies like Lodis make handbags that look like chic totes but are as practically organized as any briefcase—some even including laptop compartments—for well under $300.

The perfect purse needs to be big enough to contain your résumé and possibly samples of your work, and should be at least the size of a messenger bag or tote. Preferably it will be made of leather, but if you're opposed to that, very high quality nylon or other synthetic fabric will do. Solid colors are best, but a subtle print or texture could also work well. If you're going to show drawings, designs, spreadsheets, or plans, you need a large portfolio that is not made of cardboard. Large designer logos, even if they're Louis Vuitton or Chanel, are not appropriate.

As a journalist, when I go on a job interview I always bring along extra copies of my résumé, color copies of my print work, a DVD with my on-air reel, copies of some of the books I've written, and a screen grab of my personal blog and other works I have on the Internet. I also like to have room to take along my laptop, just in case wireless is available and I want to show something else I've done online. Once I've landed the job, I take out the work samples and sub in a recording device and my Amazon Kindle just in case I have to wait somewhere and I want to read a few chapters. I like to keep my business bag separate from my weekend and recreational purses, so it doesn't wear out quickly and so I feel like I'm a true professional when I'm on the job.

Don't despair if you're on a budget—a savvy shopper can still look fabulous for pennies on the dollar. You can find great buys on professional wear on sale at the right time of year, at designer outlets, and on various websites. My own personal work style is creative chic, and my favorite budget resources for business attire include Bloomingdales, Nordstrom, and Saks sales, where these days you can get designer clothes for up to 80 percent off. Online I like Zappos, which is not just for shoes and bags anymore but carries some chic clothing items as well, and never charges you postage, either to receive or return items—I often order the same item in a couple of different sizes, then return the ones that don't fit.

I'm a little reluctant to admit this, but I've even gotten some great buys on designer clothes on eBay. Did you know you can get brand-new, *with tags* Dianne Von Furstenberg dresses on eBay for less than half of what they'd cost you in a department store? It's true.

Best Rejuvenating Secrets from Hollywood Experts

Hollywood is the cruelest of towns. It may be true that "if I can make it there, I'll make it anywhere" in New York, but that song is talking more about personal accomplishments than physical attributes. In Los Angeles, it's all about the look. Hollywood has a reputation for frowning upon anyone who isn't at the top of their game, physically speaking, no matter how much they've accomplished. It takes a massive amount of self-confidence and assurance just to step outside to walk your dog in the morning, unless you're fully made up and wearing designer athletic wear. (Being supremely confident women, my studio executive friend Susan and I sometimes don't even comb our hair when we walk our dogs in the morning, but we usually make it back inside before the sun comes up.)

Now, if someone can be considered a top beauty expert here in Los Angeles, you know they have to be just about the best there is. I've selected two of L.A.'s finest, not only because of their credentials, but because my friends and I have had amazing experiences with them both: Dr. Gary Motykie, an award-winning, board-certified plastic surgeon who has been featured on E! Entertainment's *Dr. 90210*, and Louisa Maccan-Graves, probably one of the most photographed women in showbiz, an international beauty and rejuvenation expert and author of the doctor-recommended book *Hollywood Beauty Secrets: Remedies to the Rescue*.

When I first met Louisa a few years ago, I interviewed her for an article I was writing for a women's magazine. I guessed her age to be in the late twenties, partially because her skin, body, and hair are flawless, but also because of her vibrant positive energy. It's not for me to reveal her age, but let's just say my guess was "a few" years off. Louisa is a body parts model using her hands, stomach, lips, arms, back, and even her belly button to double for A-list celebrities including Jennifer Garner, Debra Messing, Penelope Cruz, Kate Walsh, Alyssa Milano,

Kristin Nuss Farrand was a stay-at-home mother of three until divorce edged her back into the workplace. She'd like to use the photography and fund-raising skills she's developed over the years on behalf of a nonprofit organization for seriously ill children.

Sonya Ede has spent most of her professional life in the public relations department of a major corporation. She recently took advantage of an opportunity to strike out on her own, and needs a fresh, creative, and unique image as the head of her new firm.

Air Force lieutenant colonel Susan Merrick spent twenty-two years in uniform, serving the country as an architectural engineer building military health facilities. Now the mother of two is looking for work in the private sector and doesn't have a thing to wear.

Kristin before.

Kristin's monochromatic brown locks get red highlights that will bring out the fire and creativity in her hair and her personality.

Rejuvenation expert Louisa Maccan-Graves of Hollywood Beauty Secrets gives Kristin a refreshing homemade papaya mask (see recipe, page 89).

An eyebrow gel applied with a circular brush, rather than a pencil, gives a more subtle and satisfying appearance.

Kristin after.

Sonya before.

First up for Sonya is getting the gray out, which, she and Lisa note, is a necessary step for most women over thirty.

A good straightening session with a flat-iron can achieve a low-maintenance look that will last for days.

The right foundation for
business professionals is
so sheer and natural you
hardly know it's there.

Sonya after.

Susan before.

Susan had never had her hair done professionally, so the equivalent of a squadron was called in, headed by Suburbia Salon owner Jennifer Nash.

Susan needed enough color to brighten her look, but not so much that it would frighten her husband and children.

Makeup specialist Marie Monet uses a light foundation to even skin tones, and natural yet fresh colors on eyes and lips.

Susan after.

Clothes, hair, and makeup are just the beginning of career comebacks for Susan, Sonya, and Kristin. They will go on to Botox their résumés, revitalize their online images, and fully utilize social networks to find work they love. Looking great makes them feel great and gives them the confidence they need to attract clients and employers alike. Style can be empowering.

Photos by Mary Ann Halpin / Lisa's fashions provided by select Carlisle Collection consultants (see pages 224–225) / Makeover fashions courtesy of Nordstrom stylist Jayani Clarke / Bags provided by Lodis (Lodis.com)

Cindy Crawford, Milla Jovovich, Rachel Weisz, Gwyneth Paltrow, Paulina Porizkova, and many others. That finger that pokes the Pillsbury Doughboy in the tummy? It's Louisa's.

People who travel in such big Hollywood circles are often self-absorbed and disdainful of the less glamorous, but not Louisa. Ever willing to share, she wrote *Hollywood Beauty Secrets* then developed a website around it, called HollywoodBeautySecrets.com, where she offers a free newsletter and many of the products she recommends, at budget-friendly prices.

The book and corresponding website were a brilliant business idea, incidentally, because everyone knows a modeling career can't last forever. You've seen many former models fade away into obscurity and resent it for the rest of their lives, or have extreme plastic surgery done in a desperate effort to cling to their looks. But Louisa is the perfect example of how you can make your experience work for you, rather than against you, by setting up your own Web-based business, and capitalizing on the expertise and wisdom you've established over the years.

"Whether you're looking for a new job or simply wanting to feel and look your best, you can make the choice to be happy and feel beautiful, starting now," says Louisa. "Sure, we all have a few wrinkles and pounds that we struggle with now and then. But this doesn't mean we can't change our thoughts and love who we are, beginning this very moment. Studies prove that when you look and feel your best, you become more confident and achieve more in life. All it takes is a little 'attitude adjustment.' That attitude adjustment will also make you a lot more fun to be around!"

I always feel prettier and more energetic after talking to Louisa, which says a lot about her own attitude—usually women with her physical virtues and gifts make the rest of us feel frumpy, schlumpy, and hopeless. But when Louisa heard I was writing this book, she was eager to share some of her best rejuvenating tips. Louisa is not big on costly surgical procedures or treatments, but she highly recommends these extremely cost-effective tweaks and noninvasive practices. Here are some of Louisa's top age-proofing tips, and readers can find more, as well as most of the products she mentions—at greatly reduced prices—on her website, HollywoodBeautySecrets.com. (See the resource guide for more information.)

For Your Mood

If you're over forty it's perfectly natural for you to feel blue, hopeless, overwhelmed, tired, or irritable on occasion—it's the natural result of our lives being busier and more complicated at this stage, and it also might be how our hormones roll. The good news is there are many safe supplements and practical solutions that can help you address these emotions naturally, and most can be found at your local health food store. It's always a good idea to check with your doctor before you add any supplements to your diet, but you might try adding:

- **Essential fatty acids (EFAs)** that combine fish, flaxseed, borage, and evening primrose oil are highly recommended to lift your mood, assist weight loss, promote clear thinking, improve memory, help slow down aging, hydrate skin and hair, balance hormones, decrease night sweats and hot flashes, and support vascular health, joint care, healthy blood pressure, and much more. Find this blend at vitamin or health food stores for about $12.

- **Pantothenic acid (vitamin B$_5$)** is an excellent supplement for adrenal support and mood lifting. It also helps food turn into energy. If you're exhausted or have a high-stress job, consider taking pantothenic acid daily. Find it naturally in eggs, bananas, beans, raw vegetables, and nuts.

- **Hyaluronic acid (HA)** supplements help lubricate stiff joints, rejuvenate skin and eyes, and enhance the immune system. As we age HA production slows down. A daily dose can also hydrate the skin and help slow down deteriorating eyesight.

For Your Skin

- **Exfoliate.** As we age, natural skin cell regeneration slows down (about every forty-eight days). By manually exfoliating skin two to three times a week you encourage new cells to quickly surface, reduce age spots, unclog and refine enlarged pores, smooth fine lines and wrinkles, stimulate collagen and elastin production, and even prevent sagging skin and ingrown hairs.

> Louisa recommends an enzyme peel recipe for all skin types:
> Cut a ripe papaya in half. Scoop out the seeds and pulp. Rub the inside of the papaya peel onto face, focusing under eyes, on crow's-feet area, temples, on lips, around mouth, on neck, chest, and hands. Place produce bags over hands. Wait about 20 minutes, then rinse off papaya with tepid water.

Papaya enzymes gently exfoliate and brighten skin, remove impurities, and help heal blemishes. Spas charge about $65 and up for an enzyme peel, but Louisa's budget-friendly recipe costs about $3.

■ **Use sunscreen.** *The* worst skin-aging culprit of all is exposure to the sun. Apply SPF 15 sunscreen daily, and SPF 30 if living in a sunny climate. You can also wear sunglasses, a wide-brimmed visor or hat, a long-sleeved shirt, and gloves if you like to spend time walking, exercising, or working outside. Louisa's favorite sunscreen is Neutrogena Sensitive Skin (SPF 30).

■ **Apply a daily antioxidant and a peptide.** For maximum age-proofing results, apply a facial antioxidant product in the morning and a peptide-rich product at night before bed. Antioxidants help nourish and protect skin from free radicals. Peptides are clinically documented to stimulate collagen and reduce the depth of lines and wrinkles. Antioxidant cream Aging Eraser (100 percent natural and preservative-free) and peptide-rich Perfect RX Night Serum (over 30 percent peptides) are two of the most potent, affordable products Louisa has uncovered to date.

■ **Red LED light therapy (light-emitting diode).** Noninvasive and affordable, LEDs reduce skin degradation; plump and smooth skin texture; reduce lines, wrinkles, crow's-feet, and age spots; repair damaged collagen; plump lips; help reduce inflammation; and can even help manage pain. These lights, like most other products mentioned in this section, are available at a discount on HollywoodBeautySecrets.com.

For Your Jowls and Neck

A sagging neck and jowls can be quick to give away your age. To help tone and tighten these areas, try this facial exercise: Pull your lips in and wrap them around your upper and lower teeth, then try to smile and hold for thirty seconds; repeat five to ten times. A jowl-toning device Louisa recommends is the FacialFlex Ultra for under $30 at QVC.com. To instantly tighten sagging neck skin, find Mark Traynor's Miracle Neck Lift for under $20 at HollywoodBeautySecrets.com.

For Your Smile

A winning smile gives a positive first impression. Thinning lips, yellow or stained teeth, lines around the mouth, or the wrong shade of lipstick or dark lip liner can age you.

- **Lips.** As we age, our lips become thinner as collagen production slows. Exfoliating lips as well as fine lines around the mouth can help rejuvenate these areas. LED light therapy also plumps lips and reduces lines around the mouth. Affordable lip plumping products like Sally Hansen Lip Blush Plumping Balm also works well. Lip gloss looks more youthful than lipstick and lip liner. Try a fleshy pink or berry-tinted lip gloss and skip the lip liner.

- **Teeth.** Why have yellow teeth that scream "old, outdated, and unhealthy" when it's so easy to have a fresh, vibrant smile? There are plenty of whitening products out there that you can get over-the-counter or from your dentist. Or, you can swish a mouthful of one part hydrogen peroxide and one part water for immediate results. This will help your breath, too.

For Your Eyes

If you're prone to eye puffiness in the morning, try applying a drop of emu oil (available at health food stores) under your eyes before bed. Also, avoid drinking beverages about two hours before bedtime, and sleep with an extra pillow propping up your head to prevent fluids from settling under the eyes. Smooth crow's-feet with LED light therapy or try applying Topical Refill Wrinkle Filler, a skin tightener and wrinkle filler that lasts for six to eight hours.

For Your Hands

Hands can also give your age away, so it's important to keep them looking their best. Wear lined rubber gloves when doing all housework, from dishes to dusting—even laundry. Before you go to bed apply an antioxidant or peptide-rich cream or serum on your hands and massage—apply a drop of emu oil over the top. Once a week, massage nails and push cuticles back with olive oil, then dip hands, palms up, into warm milk for about fifteen to twenty minutes. The lactic acid in milk helps exfoliate skin and fades age spots. The fat in milk moisturizes hands. And remember that subtlety is in right now. Bright or dark colors on long nails can be distracting. Neutral colors on shorter nails look fresh and professional. Sally Hansen No Chip 10-Day Nail Color in Tuff Buff is a good choice.

For Your Hair

Thinning, falling, dull, and damaged hair can happen to the best of us. For healthy, lustrous, thicker hair, consume foods rich in protein and healthy oils including essential fatty acids, fish, olive and grapeseed oil, and nuts. Include a variety of colorful vegetables, fruits, and whole grains in your diet. Choose gentle shampoos that moisturize. Sodium lauryl sulfate (SLS), found in almost all shampoos, can fade and strip color, cause dull, dry, brittle hair, and can even damage the scalp or cause falling hair. Doctor-recommended, SLS-free shampoo and conditioner by Your Crown & Glory works well.

Try Louisa's monthly hair conditioning pack recipe: Combine ½ mashed avocado, 1 slightly beaten egg, and ¼ cup olive oil. Shampoo hair first. Apply mixture on wet hair. Put on a shower cap. Leave on for 30 minutes. To boost penetration, warm a towel in a dryer and wrap the warm towel over the shower cap. (Incidentally, I use this on occasion, and although my husband makes fun of me, it works amazingly well.)

For Your Body

If only we had the stamina and imperviousness we enjoyed in college! With that energy and the wisdom we've accumulated over the years, we could conquer the world! But unfortunately, the older we get, the more care we have to take with our metabolism. It's a well-known fact that what you put in your body affects what your body looks like on the outside, and you already know the benefits of high-fiber foods, veggies, beans, lots of protein, and good fats like those found in avocados, olives, almonds, and salmon. But I bet you don't know that there's a way to safely flatten your tummy, help dissolve fat, and diminish bloating and water retention in just two weeks.

Try whipping up Louisa's doctor-approved, simple slimming tonic recipe: Add 1 tablespoon of organic apple cider vinegar to a glass of water. With this mixture, take two 100 mg capsules of kyolic (odorless) garlic oil capsules and drink before each meal. You'll banish bloating and may even drop a dress size in two to four weeks.

This combination helps cleanse the liver so it can metabolize fat more efficiently, clears blemish-prone skin, and even boosts your immune system. Or try taking green tea extract supplements on an empty stomach in the morning and before lunch to jump-start your metabolism. Green tea capsules are loaded with antioxidants that can help protect from disease and stimulate collagen production to keep skin looking firm and more youthful.

Of course exercise is important too: Did you know that weight resistance exercises can help increase the production of natural growth hormone, which slows down aging? Add about thirty minutes of aerobic exercise five times a week, and get seven to eight hours of sleep per night, and you'll slow down the aging process *and* lose weight.

When Only a Doctor Will Do

Some of us get to the point where we need to avail ourselves of a little outside professional help to actually look as young and lively as we feel. While I personally have been reluctant to go under the knife or the needle, I'm not ruling it out. The plastic surgeons I've interviewed over the years—and believe me, their numbers are legion—have told me that I'd be astonished at the number of great-looking women who have had a little work done. It appears that all the best (looking) people are doing it. Cosmetic procedures these days involve so much more than your basic nose jobs, boob jobs, and facelifts. I say that if you can afford them and they make you feel good, why not?

Dr. Motykie says that when it comes to cosmetic procedures, "less is more. You never want to err on the side of being overdone. A professional woman doesn't want to be sitting in a meeting with the people across from her thinking, 'Hey, nice facelift!' or 'I wonder what she had done to her face?' What you *do* want is for people to be saying, 'Wow! She looks great! So relaxed and confident!'"

To stay within that realm, there are a number of simple, less aggressive procedures that can easily be done during your lunch break, and can make years of difference. They include:

Botox. This is by far the most popular procedure, according to Dr. Motykie. It's for the woman who notices a few lines on her face, and is feeling as if "the dew is off the rose," so to speak. Botox works, and is a great way to give someone a rested look, at the same time removing wrinkles, he says. He also notes that it can actually improve your expression. If done right, rather than freezing your forehead, it can erase the lines that make you look grumpy and/or tired. "It can help you look a little more enthusiastic and energetic," he says. The most common places for Botox injections are around the eyes to erase crow's-feet and open the eyes a bit; in the space between the eyes to erase angry-looking lines; and in the forehead, which can give a softer, more relaxed look. The first injections can last from three to five months, but it has a cumulative effect, and Botox injections can eventually last upwards of six months if done regularly prior to that.

Fillers: These procedures can also be done during your lunch break. Rather than paralyzing muscles like Botox, fillers erase lines by directly filling them in. Most people have fillers such as Restylane, Juvéderm, and Sculptra, just to name a few, to fix lines around the mouth, to give them plumper, more youthful-looking lips, and in the nasal labial folds (the lines that run between the nose and the corners of the mouth). "You want to be extremely conservative with fillers in the lips," Dr. Motykie cautions. The last thing you need is that unattractive duckbill look you see on so many desperate celebrities.

Peels and/or lasers. We've come a long way since the days of the peel that would leave you looking like a scalded chicken and take three weeks to heal. Now these too can be done as lunchtime procedures. They can rejuvenate the surface of the skin, even out the color, texture, and pigment—even remove sun damage. "They can achieve brighter, healthier, more glowing skin," says Dr. Motykie, adding that they can also remove some fine lines or wrinkles, but they're mostly for color and tightening. There are many types of lasers that do different things—some take the red out of your skin, some remove veins, others tighten and lighten the skin, and some can even remove tattoos (which is a very popular procedure right now—every time I see Angelina Jolie in person these days, it seems like she has a little less ink. She used to be covered. I think it's a good choice for her). These procedures used to be called "resurfacing," but now they're referred to as "rejuvenation." Rather than removing a layer of skin from the entire face, the process now pixelates certain areas, which leads to faster healing, contracting, and tightening. The technology is moving forward so quickly that it's hard to keep up with it.

Then there are the procedures that require minor surgery and anesthesia. If they're done for cosmetic purposes, a hospital stay is completely unnecessary. Most can be done in a couple of hours in a surgical center. Among these procedures are:

Fat grafting. As some people get older, explains Dr. Motykie, they lose fat in the face and start looking hollow and gaunt. This can be remedied by borrowing a little fat from the belly, back, or under the chin and putting it in the face, usually under the eyes, in the cheeks and lips, or under the nasal labial lines. "This can make you look younger and softer, but it's hard for people to discern exactly what you had done," he says. About half the fat will dissipate over a six-month time period, but the other half usually stays put. Dr. Motykie notes that fat has stem cells in it, and he feels it rejuvenates the skin from the inside out and adds natural estrogen. He usually replaces the fat in the face by working from inside the mouth, so there are no scars on the face.

Blepharoplasty. If the eyes are the window to the soul, they can often give away just how much time that soul has seen. Age often shows up first in the eyes. Heaviness of the upper eyelid as well as bags under the eyes can be fixed with minor surgery called blepharoplasty. A small incision in the crease of the upper eyelid can heal within a week. For the lower eyes Dr. Motykie recommends going in from inside the eyelid and removing the little baggies so no scar is visible. These procedures, along with a little laser work to remove the crepe-like surface under the eyes, can completely rejuvenate the eye area.

Graduating up to more complicated and less subtle surgeries, there are procedures such as facelifts and brow lifts that can require weeks of recovery time. But perhaps the most popular and effective now, according to Dr. Motykie, is the breast lift. He says it gives women a more youthful, less matronly look, and improves their posture to make them look healthier, stronger, and more energetic. Breast enhancement can achieve the same effects for the less well endowed, if it is not overdone.

"Of course, a little bit of maintenance along the way will prevent major surgery later," says Dr. Motykie when discussing these procedures. Certainly none of them are standard operating procedure nor absolute requirements for women over thirty-five. It all has to do with attitude. If you feel better, you look better, and that's the bottom line.

NEWS FLASH ON THE LASH!

I've never been one to run out and try the latest and purportedly greatest cosmetic procedures, but I was attending a luncheon at Bob Hope's former and Justin Timberlake's current country club recently, and I heard plastic surgeon Dr. Robert Orloff talk about Latisse, a new, FDA-approved product from Allergan that actually makes your eyelashes grow in darker, thicker, and longer. His assistant was with him, and she said Latisse had made her eyelashes grow so long she actually had to trim them!

Knowing that thinning, pale, stubby lashes are a sure sign of aging and that thick, lush lashes are as hot and hip as can be, I decided to try it. We blondies, especially, have trouble with disappearing lashes as we age. I ran right down to Dr. Orloff's office the next day and began the Latisse treatment, which involves brushing on the clear liquid like eyeliner every night before you go to bed. Within two weeks I started to notice a difference, and within four weeks everyone else did. Now, one coat of mascara and a quick crimp of the eyelash curler, and I get a better look than I ever did with false eyelashes. Seriously, this stuff is incredible.

It must be doctor prescribed, however. To find one near you who can prescribe it, go to Latisse.com and use the Find a Doctor Tool, or call 1-800-433-8871.

Now that you're not only feeling your best but also looking your best, it's time to go out there and show off your fresh, hip self. You don't just want to find potential employers, you want potential employers to find you, and to know exactly what you're about the second they see you. This can be achieved with some resourceful personal branding, and you'll be getting a crash course on it in the next chapter.

5

Create a *Brand* New You

If you can, be first. If you can't be first, create a new
category in which you can be first.

—*Al Ries and Jack Trout,*
The 22 Immutable Laws of Marketing

Branding is not just for cattle and corporations anymore—it's also
for savvy job seekers like you, who want to stand out from all the
other candidates and make a real statement. Smart, directed individual
branding can help you leave a memorable impression on employers that
they just can't shake. All the "best" people brand, from Oprah to Barack
Obama to Martha Stewart to J. K. Rowling—hey, Madonna rebrands or
recreates herself every couple of years. This chapter will help you think
of yourself and present yourself as the one-of-a-kind, talented, distinctive package that you are.

This is where personal expression becomes professional: **Every
potential employer out there should know what you consistently
stand for and how you are different from the rest**. You don't have to be
all things to all people. But you do have to be exceptional, memorable,
and outstanding in at least one area of your choosing. While many of
you are Renaissance women who excel at a wide variety of endeavors,
when presenting yourself for a certain job or position, you should pick
your greatest asset and make yourself into the poster child for it. You're
not just a CEO, you're the CEO who can trim the fat and cut budgets
in half. You're not just a marketing expert, you're the marketing expert
who knows how to pinpoint your products' demographic and grab it by
the throat.

A great example of this is the Honorable Sherrill Ellsworth. She is not just an attorney. She is a specialist in family law as it pertains to domestic violence and child abuse. She is now a California state supervising judge who is in demand all over the country as a legal speaker and educator. She's been a dear friend of mine since first grade, and her story has always inspired me. A straight-A student and class president, she stunned us all when she left high school a year early—she wanted to get married and start a family (in that order) and finish school while she was raising kids. That she did—she earned her undergrad and her law degree and started her own legal practice while raising six children! She tried some very high-profile, nationally known cases, and dabbled in various types of law, but it was family law that truly drew her in. So many of her colleagues gravitated toward more high-profile, high-salaried legal fields, but perhaps because she was a mother herself and had seen so many different sides of life, she found her calling in family law. She garnered expertise by volunteering and serving on pro bono committees and boards. Sherrill branded herself as the go-to person for all family legal issues.

"Anyone can become an expert," she says, when talking about how to distinguish yourself from the rest and create your own brand. "Volunteering is a good place to start, and you won't be the only one who benefits from it." And you don't have to be an attorney to help victims of domestic violence or child abuse, she reminds us. "You can volunteer at a shelter, you can help raise funds, you can become an advocate, you can be a receptionist at a service center." It is possible to get almost any kind of experience and expertise you need in almost any field if you stick your pinky toe in the water and volunteer. And some volunteer positions actually pay.

It's all about finding your true niche and making it known. Each of us finds our true passion in our own unique way. It took a catastrophe to lead Anna Nicholas to her niche. She had a law degree and had been successful in a number of professional endeavors, but in her mid-forties she was still pursuing her dream of becoming an Olympic equestrian. She was long-listed for the U.S. team, but, she says, "I knew I should have been out of that. Something told me not to go on." But still she persisted. It was extremely difficult for her to leave her passion behind, even though her heart and head told her it was time to move on. Finally her body convinced her: She fell off her horse and broke her back. She was a single mother with a school-aged son to look after at the time, and had to face the music. "I finally *had* to give up my dream of being on the U.S. Equestrian team," she said. But she wasn't through with the sport altogether.

Once she'd healed, she looked around for a way to combine her profession (law) with her passion, equestrianism. She noted that there are plenty of legal issues in the equestrian world—with vets, breeders, boarders, trainers, owners, riders, ranchers, instructors, competitions, and organizations. With so many different negotiations and contracts involved, there were bound to be disagreements. So Anna decided to brand herself as an equestrian mediator. It's an admittedly narrow field, but so narrow that she doesn't have a lot of competition. A website describing her services, EqADR.com, as well as her networking efforts at numerous equestrian events such as shows, competitions, and festivals, put her well on her way. "Once I got past the fact that I was giving up my dream," she says, "I was able to heal and merge my passion with my profession."

Anna notes that her self-created position as a legal mediator for equestrian matters can mostly be taken care of while her son is at school, and she's free afterward to watch him pursue his own passion, tennis. "There are plenty of businesses you can get involved in that allow you that luxury," she says. "Some people cook, others do crafts, some people make beautiful gift baskets." It's all a matter of finding that sweet spot where your passion and your profession meet.

In-House Branding

Suppose you're perfectly happy in your own company and have no interest in starting your own business. It's a promotion you're seeking—you want to climb the corporate ladder from the inside. Personal branding is still very important to help you stand out from the rest of your colleagues.

Julie Huang, for example, was employed by a major corporation with many different departments, and had gone just about as far as she possibly could in hers, simply because everyone else above her had seniority and wasn't planning on going anywhere. All her colleagues had satisfying work, and the corporation treated them well. But being an ambitious person who likes a challenge, Julie needed to grow—she needed to move up. So she took a look at her talents and passions and created her own niche within her corporate environment: She proposed creating her own department that met the needs of all the other departments and utilized her own unique skills. Julie was a logistics wizard: She could manage events, materials, transportation; everything from soup to nuts. Yet each department in her company took care of their own logistics. Julie suggested setting up a department that would handle all the details for everyone else. It seems she was one of the few people in her company who actually enjoyed working with the details. To everyone else they were a major pain, and her colleagues were more than happy to get them off their plates and pass them over to Julie. Needless to say, her proposal was wildly popular and well-received. Voilà! Everyone is now happier than ever, free to concentrate on the tasks they love best, and Julie is on the fast track to becoming the vice president of a department she created. Incidentally, much of her work can be done from her home office, and her company is no longer requiring her to spend forty hours a week at corporate headquarters. This benefits everyone on many different levels.

PROFESSIONAL ADVICE

Lisa Narvas, a lead systems analyst with a large, global corporation, has always been very happy with her company, but being the sharp, growth-oriented individual she is, she can't help but feel the desire to improve herself and her position. She recently earned a major promotion, and offers the following self-branding advice for moving up within an organization or company:

1. Keep learning. Stay on top of the major trends in your industry; what your competitors are doing, and what regulations are coming down the pike that may impact your industry. Take classes, read publications, participate in webinars and professional groups, and obtain relevant certifications for your field.

2. Be a team player. Treat everyone with respect and courtesy: The backstabbing witch who is your peer today may be your boss tomorrow, and administrative assistants are gatekeepers to leaders and resources you need. Give credit to the team, don't grab all the glory for yourself. Send thank-you notes and/or give little gifts to people who do a good job or go out of the way to help you.

3. Be flexible. Never, ever say, "That's not in my job description," or "We've always done it this way." Always look for a better, faster, cheaper, more efficient way to do everything, then document it and share it. Be willing to take on new tasks. Volunteer to help overloaded colleagues, especially if they are working on a high-profile project.

4. Become visible. In a large company, you need to find ways to stand out. Get as much face time as you can with your leader, your leader's leader, and other VIPs as appropriate. This can be accomplished by participating in skip level meetings, open presentations, town halls, team-building events, and community volunteer events. Better still, organize and/or lead a team-building or volunteer event, the broader the audience the better.

5. Network. You never know when you may need to look for a new job or obtain some type of specific information from a former colleague. Maintain contacts with people you've worked with, from every company you've worked for, and from every charity or community organization you're involved in. Tools such as LinkedIn and Twitter make this a fairly easy task. Participate in trade organizations, don't just carry the membership card around in your wallet.

Lisa emphasizes that in the tech field, how you perform is far more important than how you look. Still, it's a good idea to know how to present yourself when you run into colleagues in the workplace or out in public. That's why the "elevator pitch" is so important, whether you're looking to move up, move out, or move along, professionally speaking.

The All-Important Elevator Pitch

One of the most important aspects of personal branding is the ability to summarize yourself and what you do in twenty seconds or less. This is known as the Elevator Pitch, because if people ask you, while you're in an elevator, what you do, you can give them an accurate idea before they reach their floor. There are infinite uses for elevator pitches, such as at any kind of social or professional gathering where introductions are necessary, or just about anytime anyone asks you who you are and what you do. Seriously, how many times have you been asked, "And what do you do?" Do you have a quick, interesting answer, or do you respond with, "Oh, I'm just a..." or "I work at..." How memorable and representative is that? Sales reps frequently use elevator pitches to promote products and services, so why not write one to pitch the most valuable product in your possession: you?

The elevator pitch is somewhat of a fine art. If you don't have a few quick, concise sentences prepared, it's far too easy to ramble and lose your audience, especially today, when so many of us wear so many hats. For example, when someone asks me what I do, if I weren't prepared, my inclination would be to say something like:

"Well, my name is Lisa Johnson...Lisa Johnson Mandell...I recently got married and added my husband's name, and sometimes I forget to use it...I'm a journalist by trade, focusing on career image and entertainment, and I do broadcast as well as print and new media... which means I do on-air work for television and radio, I create content for the Internet and I write for newspapers and magazines... I'm also a film critic...I interview a lot of movie stars...but I write books too...I've written books on relationships and professional image and trying to help people find jobs they love...and I also do public speaking and consulting…so I guess you could add self-help author and speaker…"

Sheesh! I get bored and confused just writing that. In the time it would take to get all that out, my new acquaintance's eyes would have glazed over and you would practically see the thought bubble popping up asking, "When are we going to get to my damn floor?"

I get a much better response when I say:

"I'm Lisa Johnson Mandell, a film critic, author, and multimedia journalist who's used Hollywood experience to help people revitalize themselves and find jobs they love in these tough economic times."

You can imagine how that piques instant interest from everyone in the elevator.

The mission statement you wrote in chapter 1 (see page 30) is a good place to start when composing your own elevator pitch. Remember to be concise and all-encompassing. If the person you're talking to wants to know about more about your specific skills, you'll be asked to elaborate. Also, your elevator pitch doesn't need to include the fact that you're looking for work. Work will find *you* if your pitch is intriguing enough. I can't tell you how many times I've been sitting in a theater and, in chatting with the stranger sitting by my side, heard the magic words, "I'm a freelance entertainment writer and I just got a killer interview with…" At which point I ask them for their card, telling them that I could use that interview on my website. That quick elevator pitch could be worth several hundred dollars in your pocket immediately, or even more down the line, if it leads to landing you a job.

PROFESSIONAL ADVICE

A good elevator pitch includes the following elements:

1. An introduction (your name)
2. Your profession
3. What needs you meet
4. What makes you different from everyone else

Even people with simple, straightforward careers and professions can benefit from an elevator pitch. A first-grade teacher can say, "My name is Molly and I'm an elementary school teacher," leaving no impression whatsoever, or she can say, "My name is Molly Woo. I'm a first-grade teacher at Washington Elementary and I specialize in accelerating reading skills."

With an elevator pitch like that, she'll have the entire car listening, with half the people in it handing her business cards and inquiring, "My kid needs tutoring, are you available?" Even if you're perfectly happy with your current job, a good elevator pitch can bring new opportunities, and maybe even get you a little lucrative work on the side.

Don't worry about sounding vain or self-promoting. The elevator pitch is a response to a question. Most people won't expect that kind of concise yet intriguing detail, and will be fascinated and impressed when they receive it.

Do worry, however, if you're having a hard time coming up with something unique about your skills and abilities. Surely you have some. If not, I'd suggest developing some quickly. And if you're in a "filler" job at the moment, you don't need to mention it. Even if you're currently working as a barista at Starbucks, that doesn't change the fact that you're also an interior designer who integrates simple green principles into living spaces, for example.

Public speaking professionals suggest that you make your elevator pitch sound conversational—use contractions, such as "I'm," "we're," "that's," and so on. Don't let it sound memorized or canned. Also, it's best to keep it short and sweet—eliminate superfluous words and sentences. Pare it down to the very core or essence, so you don't ramble. Practice your speech a few times—maybe even in the mirror. This will help you remember to smile and breathe while you're speaking. Avoid industry jargon, or being too specific—your elevator pitch should be something that anyone can understand, even if they don't have a clue about your particular profession.

Once you have your general elevator pitch down, you can revise it for the occasion at hand, such as a self-introduction at a job interview, a cold call to a potential employer, when meeting someone else from the company that currently employs you, in an e-mail cover letter, at a casual networking opportunity with new acquaintances you make at places like the movies or your child's soccer game, or even a tête-à-tête with a potential romantic prospect, if you're single. It's always appreciated when you throw new acquaintances a bone by telling them who you are and giving them a little something to ask you about.

Getting Carded

It's important that you have your own personal business card to go along with your elevator pitch, even if you are unemployed. That way, if someone hears your speech, wants to contact you, and you feel that it might be a good connection, you can just whip out your card instead of having to go through the awkwardness of digging in your purse for a pen and scribbling your phone number on the back of a bank deposit receipt.

In addition, your business card is a great branding tool. It can convey quite a bit about you. If it's plain, simple, and elegant with black type on cream stock, it tells people you are a classic professional who means business. If you select something interesting and unusual, it suggests you are creative and original. If you happened to have designed your own logo for your business, by all means it should be on your business card to make it more memorable and instantly convey a little about who you are and what you do.

If the company you work for hasn't issued you a business card or if you are self-employed or unemployed, your card should state the following information:

- Name, with full name or initial, no prefix: **Eleanor J. Rigby**

- Title and/or business: Planner, **Dreamtime Weddings**

- Business address: If you work out of your home, however, and you don't want to tell any random stranger where you live, just give a geographical location, such as: **Liverpool, England.**

■ E-mail address: If your own personal e-mail address is something other than a derivation of your name, get a new business e-mail address, such as **EleanorRigby@gmail.com**, rather than **FaceInAJar@ AlltheLonelyPeople.com**.

■ Web address (if you have one): **DreamtimeWeddings.com**

■ Cell phone or business number, area code first: **555-555-5555**. *Never* give out your home phone number—you never know what kind of weirdo might get hold of your card, and a simple Google search of your phone number can reveal your home address. You can't be too careful.

If this sounds intimidating during a time when finances are tight, know that you don't have to spend a lot of money on fancy engraving. You can buy your own card stock and print your cards at home on your own computer, or even better, you can get personalized business cards online for little more than the price of postage, at sites like Stationary-Stationery.com, FreePrintableBusinessCards.net, Bizcard .com, or my own personal favorite, VistaPrint.com. They have designs customized for most specific industries, such as finance and insurance, real estate, food and beverage, beauty spa and massage, arts and entertainment, health care, politics, law and public service, and more. These companies don't just stop at business cards, but offer personalized matching stationery, address labels, even pens, T-shirts, and notes at extremely reasonable prices.

PROFESSIONAL ADVICE

Insider tips for using these printing services:

1. Never select a design from the "Most Popular" list—you want your card to be unique.

2. Pick a design or colors that reflect your profession, not your disposition, family, or hobby; in other words, unless you're a vet, no kittycats or bunnies.

3. Some sites will charge you extra if you don't want their own promo on the back of their card—pay the extra fee to have the back of the card blank. You don't want to promote someone else on your business card, and you don't want people to know you got the cards for free.

4. If matching stationery, envelopes, address labels, thank-you notes, sticky pads, and so forth are offered, you might want to spring for those as well. You can use the supplies for résumés, cover letters, and any other correspondence you might have with future employers. They will be helpful in identifying you and will immediately strengthen your brand.

I began by selecting a business card design from VistaPrint. It was a blend of pretty purples and blues, with a big, gold, stylized star on it. I thought that would be appropriate for someone in the entertainment industry. I got matching stationery and notepads, address labels, and other items, and my colleagues started identifying the graphic with me. I liked it so much that I gave it to my Web designer to incorporate the colors in the website he created for me. That, however, was before VistaPrint started offering matching websites that cost as little as $4.99 per month, depending on the features you select. There are plenty of services out there that offer comparable products. Branding yourself visually is so easy and inexpensive, there's no reason not to do it.

Fun fact

SWEET BRANDING

If you're starting your own business or trying to call out your own skills and attributes, you might have fun using the very sweet branding trick of ordering customized M&M's. At mymms.com you can chose from twenty different colors and select your own message of up to sixteen characters, two on each line. Why not put your name on some, your company or profession on others? They'll even print your face or company logo on the candies. It's not cheap, but it is fun, and a very memorable way to promote your own personal brand.

Picture Perfect

The second step in visually branding yourself is having high-quality photos of yourself taken. Even if you're camera shy and applying for a behind-the-scenes tech job, this is still an absolute must. If the thought of being in front of the camera makes you cringe, know that I hear you. I felt the same way, and it was my husband who finally convinced me that current, flattering photos were a necessity. "People need to be able to *see* how fresh and vibrant you are. Words on paper can't express that," he told me. I saw his point. With as much experience as I had, even if I omitted some of it and deleted my college graduation dates, a potential employer might get the idea that there was a lot of mileage on this old workhorse, and couldn't tell if I was a tired old broken nag or a feisty, fresh filly. Flattering photos would immediately clear things up. Since some of the positions I was applying for were on camera, I would even be able to use the photos on my résumé. And if I was going to build my own blog site as a more graphic résumé and self-promotion vehicle, pictures were essential. I couldn't distinctly brand myself without them.

Believe it or not, having professional photos taken can even be a great confidence builder, and confidence plays a huge role in your career comeback. Your own personal image will soar when you see yourself at your very best, which is exactly how a good photographer will present you. You will be stunned to see how great you can look, and how others see you. "Hey, if I can look that good," you think, "there ain't no stoppin' me now!"

WORTH A THOUSAND WORDS

Even if you have a low-profile job and no one will see you without a mask or a uniform in the plain light of day, you can use flattering professional photos for a number of purposes, such as:

1. Your business cards. Many real estate agents use photos on their cards for good reason—it's easier to remember a face than a name, and a smile builds trust and confidence. Sales and marketing professionals, as well as people in beauty, fashion, and style industries, can benefit greatly from a beautiful picture with a smile.

2. Your website or blog. A picture is worth more than a thousand words online—it's worth a thousand hits. Your website or blog will say so much more about you and be so much more memorable with a picture on it.

3. Your online profile. If you're single and into online dating, you can use these same photos on your Web profile. And since the photos were taken for professional purposes, they're tax deductible! They're also great for Facebook and LinkedIn profiles.

4. Great gifts. They serve as cherished remembrances for family members, and did I mention they're tax deductible?

Still not feeling comfortable about smiling for the camera? I understand. Having professional photos taken was a critical step in my own career comeback, but one I was *extremely* reluctant to take. You see, I've never considered myself photogenic, and I absolutely abhor having that type of attention focused on me. Even my wedding photographers wanted to smack me for not standing still and posing long enough. Oh, I don't mind being on camera when I have something interesting or helpful to say, but I feel like an idiot just standing there baring my teeth and leering while someone makes a fuss and clicks all around me.

Besides, I had no idea what to wear or how to look. I searched professional headshots online, and found quite a few in my age range that belonged to actresses. Most had several looks, which included the Anchor Woman, the Girl Next Door, and the Vixen, and none of those were really appropriate for a nonperforming professional. Then I looked up headshots for professional women, and most of those showed sparkling smiles and squinty eyes under big helmet hair and boring business suits. Yuck! Definitely not "me" either. It was when I began looking at author photos that I started to see something I could, perhaps, endure—black turtlenecks, heads at unusual angles, interesting backgrounds. That seemed to be more my style.

Next I had to decide on clothing, which also stumped me. I knew I needed several different looks, and I'd been told a million times that big prints are bad and cool colors are good with my complexion, but beyond that I was at a loss. That's when I called in a twentysomething friend to sift through my closet and help me find some decent outfits for the photo shoot (see chapter 4).

The dreaded day of the photo shoot arrived, and my husband had to push me out the door, armed with a suitcase, garment bag, shoeboxes, and makeup carrier. I felt like such a fool. Little did I know that by the end of the day, my wonderful photographer, Mary Ann Halpin, would have to push me back out her door to go home again. I had the time of my life, and you can too.

PROFESSIONAL ADVICE

GETTING READY FOR YOUR CLOSE-UP

Here are some tips for making the most of your professional photo shoot:

1. Do your homework. Get referrals for photographers from your friends, then look at their work online. If they don't have a website, they're not up on the latest technology and you probably won't want to use them. If you can't afford a professional, ask a friend to do it, but make sure you see some of his or her work first.

2. Find a photographer who works in a private environment. You're probably self-conscious enough in front of the camera without having to worry about people driving by and honking at you, or walking by and staring, making comments, giving you devil horns, or worse. Also, no matter what someone tells you about the virtues of natural lighting, a good photographer will control the environment to present you in the absolute best light for your own coloring.

3. Get plenty of sleep the night before the shoot. Also, do something relaxing the morning of, like taking a long hot bath or drinking herbal tea. Go easy on the caffeine, which could make you even more nervous, tense, and jumpy than you already feel.

4. If you have the funds, have your makeup done professionally. If you don't have the funds, go to the cosmetics counter at a department store and have a professional do your makeup. Make sure you tell them you need a look for a photo shoot, but you want it to be as natural as possible. Buy a tube of lip gloss to make it worth their while. You can reapply it during the shoot.

5. Again, if you can afford it, have your hair professionally blown out or styled. Ideally, you can find a hair and makeup person who will do both, and will stick around with you for at least some of the shoot. My photographer recommended one to me who only charged $150 for hair and makeup, and that was one killer deal, especially here in Hollywood.

6. Make sure all financial negotiations have been taken care of prior to the shoot. You don't want to be worrying about that while you're having your picture taken. Many photographers require half the fee up front when you make the appointment, and the other half when the pictures are delivered.

7. Ask the photographer to show you some of the shots as you go. Digital photography makes this very easy. Not only will you see whether or not your photographer is getting the photos you had in mind, but it should amaze and relax you to see how wonderful you look on camera.

I was lucky enough to find a photographer who specializes in shooting strong, independent women over forty. As a matter of fact, she's created a beautiful book out of some of her photos, entitled *Fearless Women*, with each subject wielding a powerful sword. Mary Ann sat me down with a nice cup of tea and chatted with me for about twenty minutes before we started the shoot. She asked me who I was, what I liked, and had me explain the purpose of the photos. She was then able to make me feel like an absolute goddess as I was posing. She knew who I was, knew exactly how I wanted to appear, and took photos of me that have appeared in newspapers, books, magazines, and on television worldwide—not to mention all over the Internet. If you have any sort of compensation package from your old job, or if you have funding to start a new business, I would highly suggest using some of that money to have professional photos taken.

If you don't have the money to spend on a professional photo shoot, get a friend who is good with a digital camera to set up your own private studio session following the advice I've given above. You definitely need to put a fresh face on your own personal brand. Besides, photos are absolutely essential for the best personal branding tool of all, your own blog or website, which we'll dive into in the next chapter.

6

Shine Online

Everyone is entitled to my opinion.

—Madonna

Regardless of your age, profession, or position in life, your own personal blog is an absolute must-have in today's excruciatingly competitive job market. Available for anyone to view, anywhere, anytime, it not only sets you apart and helps you appear fresh and current, but will also make it possible for potential employers to find and contact you. Why not allow them to make the first move? And oh, the networking you'll be able to do! Think of it: The second you start your own blog, you will immediately have something in common with the estimated 100 million other bloggers worldwide—that's one major network!

To some, starting a website or blog may sound complicated, intimidating, and expensive. But honestly, if you take the time to look into it, you'll find it's amazingly simple, can even be done for free, and surprise, surprise, it just might turn out to be a lot of fun for you!

What's the difference between a website and a blog, you may ask? Well, a standard website could contain your pictures, videos, résumé, bio, and contact information. A blog is sort of a running commentary, written by you, you and only you. It comes from the term "weblog," so in essence it's a sort of a personal log posted on the Web. Your personal website *must* contain a blog if you want to get noticed. Of course there are websites out there—government, educational, and retail, for example—that don't contain blogs, but these are purely informational and not at all promotional. It's up to you whether you host your blog on your own personal website, which will also allow you room to post photos, your résumé, and any other pertinent information about yourself, or you post your blog on another site dedicated to blogging, which allows you to take advantage of the traffic that's already coming to the established blog site. Whichever you choose, there are myriad professional advantages to making your Web presence known, which include:

1. Show potential employers how Web savvy you are.

2. Highlight skills, experience, and other assets too numerous to list on your résumé.

3. Keep communication skills sharp. No matter what your field, written communication skills are essential, especially in this day and age of e-mails and blogs. Updating your site will give you plenty of practice.

4. Showcase your beautiful mug. Show the world how vibrant and professional you are and let them get to know you a little better by posting the flattering photos you've had taken. If you're in a field where putting your photo on your résumé is not appropriate, this is a way for potential employers to get a visual image of you.

5. Give employers an opportunity to find you. Many businesses do Web searches now to locate new talent.

6. Keep in touch with old friends and business associates. They can read your blog so you won't have to send out individual e-mails to everyone.

7. Keep you current in your field by encouraging you to search for interesting blog material on the latest and greatest developments in your area on a weekly, if not daily, basis.

8. Further define and identify your own personal, unique brand.

9. Earn you a little extra money. Don't expect to make millions overnight, but Google ads and associations with companies like

Amazon.com, Netflix.com, and Zappos.com, where you get a percentage of the price if a link from your site leads to a sale, can buy you lunch every now and then.

10. Have fun. Blogging is just one more creative outlet for you. Who knows? It might become a favorite new hobby.

What to Write About

What will your site contain? Anything and everything that you are passionate about and that focuses on you *as a professional.* I stress "as a professional" because a lot of people use their personal sites as a sort of public scrapbook, since they're not comfortable writing about themselves. The first thing it might occur to them to post is an item about their kids, their pets, or their travels. That's the kind of personal information that is much better posted on MySpace, Facebook, or a social site of that nature. Your professional blog should contain your own opinions and observations about your niche in the field you have chosen. It can also contain information you've read on other sites or blogs, if you provide a link and give them full credit.

Think of it as a place to position yourself as an expert and commentator on the subject of your choice. Career coach Kay Stout has done an exceptional job of this on her blog Another Point of View (http://anotherpointofview.typepad.com). While she doesn't have a picture of herself posted, she does post frequent, fabulous insights on job searching, and she often quotes and links to other articles. By visiting her blog, you'll get some great job-hunting ideas, as well as see an example of a very well-written blog. I've started yet another blog myself, which gives people hope, hints, and tips for finding work in this challenging economy. You'll find it at LisaJohnsonMandell.com.

When I was first giving myself a career makeover, I wanted people to know that I was a Hollywood insider and film critic, so I decided to use the name of my radio feature, LisaLiveInHollywood.com, and post reviews, interviews, and unique news that only I could report. But you don't have to post quotes from movie stars to have an interesting blog—

you can make your blog fascinating no matter what your occupation. All real estate agents worth their salt today have websites where they feature the homes they're selling and post information about trends, neighborhoods, design ideas, gardening, etc. Teachers can blog about interesting articles and books they've read, or experiences in the classroom (always remember to change the names to protect the guilty). Medical professionals can write about interesting studies they've found online. Artists blog about their inspiration and post photos of their latest work. You'll find yourself infinitely more engaged in the world around you and receptive to new knowledge and ideas when you're constantly searching for interesting items to blog.

Building Your Web Home

The intent of my Hollywood blog was not so much to get a lot of traffic, but to brand myself as the ultimate film insider and critic. I needed a very Lisa-centric place where I could not only show the world that I am fresher and hipper than my vast amount of experience might indicate, but also make it known that I had access to the world's biggest stars. I needed a place to prominently feature myself in photos and interviews with people like Steven Spielberg, Clint Eastwood, Brad Pitt, Johnny Depp, Tom Hanks, Forest Whitaker, Emile Hirsch, Robert Downey Jr., Jodie Foster, Jack Black, Kate Hudson, Philip Seymour Hoffman—even Dr. Phil!

Because I was interested in working for a website and needed to appear original and Web savvy, I didn't use a generic, prefab template for my site. A template found online is perfect for most people, but more about that later. I needed something designed specifically for me, so I went on Craigslist.org (which is a great place to advertise your services if you're a freelancer) and I searched for Web designers whose work I found most attractive and cutting-edge. I got bids from several who appealed to me. I found a talented designer named James Richman (JamesRichman.com), who gave me what I considered to be a fair rate for the type of site I wanted.

James advised me to look on prefab template sites like

TemplateMonster.com, BuildYourSite.com, BoxedArt.com, Homestead
.com, and FreeWebsiteTemplates.com. There I picked out the types of
sites I liked, to give him an idea of the graphic style I was looking for.
If you have a decent amount of skill on your computer, you can pick a
template from any of these sites and build your own. Instructions are
clear and simple. But I was out to fortify my "LisaLiveInHollywood"
brand, so together James and I came up with the idea of using the blue
and purple night-sky colors of my business cards, a drive-in movie
screen that would have a Flash presentation of some of the pictures
I'd taken with celebrities, and an old-fashioned marquee that featured
my name with tracking lights around it. Including Flash (animation)
on your homepage is definitely an eye catcher, but also slightly complicated for the novice.

James used a fabulous system called WordPress for the backend
(technical) part of my blog site, making it so easy for me to post and
update that I was stunned. I'd heard nightmare stories about friends
having to wait for their webmasters to update their sites and pay exorbitant fees every time they wanted to change anything. Those days are
gone, thank heavens. With the systems available now, you can update
your own site anytime, anywhere, for free. WordPress even lets you
post your own 3GB blog at no charge, and you can pay extra for the
flashy add-ons, if you choose to use them.

Among other sites where you can easily (and often freely) post your
own blogs and websites are:

Blog.com. Offers free blog hosting with unlimited bandwidth and
more benefits for paid members.

Blogger.com. A great starting site to get a taste of blogging, very easy
to use.

Blogher.com. Extremely easy for beginners, and gives your blog a
home where other women can easily find you.

Blogr.com. Allows you to blog and host photos, videos, and podcasts.

BlogSpirit.com. A European-based blogging site that offers a
thirty-day trial and subscriptions thereafter.

Blogster.com. Offers free image hosting in addition to free blogs.

Bravenet.com. Free blog hosting with RSS feeds and more.

ClearBlogs.com. Free blog hosting and offers templates, friends-only posts, and more.

LiveJournal.com. Great for beginners, it offers the ability to make your blog private and allow only those you give permission to read your posts.

MovableType.org. A serious "professional publishing platform" with cool plug-ins.

Netcipia.com. A free blog and wiki for private or public display with 2GB of storage.

OpenDiary.com. Offers unlimited storage and posts and low-cost subscription rates for advanced features.

ShoutPost.com. A platform for creating blogs with a focus on generating traffic.

Squarespace.com. Lets you build your blog with numerous themes; also allows you to add other site features.

Terapad.com. Offers blogs as well as features such as an integrated store, in case you have products you'd like to sell.

Tumblr.com. An easy blog platform with a focus on allowing media-rich posts.

TypePad.com. A favorite of business executives, this is somewhat of an advanced, serious place for the professional.

Vox.com. Part of the SixApart family of blogging sites, very much geared toward the personal journal types of blogs

Weebly.com. Allows you to create a site and blog and offers free hosting and design changes on the fly.

WordPress.com. My absolute favorite free blogging site, they make it really easy for you to progress into a full-fledged site with all the bells and whistles you can imagine, all easily applicable by the neophyte.

Xanga.com. Part social network, part blogging, all free.

Yahoo360.com. This would be part of your Yahoo! account, and features really easy publishing.

Zoomshare.com. Free blog hosting with 250MB of free storage.

If nothing on this list strikes your fancy, the easiest way of all to gain a Web presence involves starting a page on a social networking site such as MySpace.com or Facebook.com. We'll discuss those more in the next chapter, but my advice would be to start pages on those sites in addition to, rather than instead of, a separate, independent blog.

Content Is Queen

So much for the nuts and bolts of your site, now let's talk about content. Your blog may have amazing graphics, but if your copy is boring, unoriginal, or sloppy, it will be a direct reflection on you and will defeat your purpose. You want to post content that others can't wait to read, and shows off your best abilities. When writing a blog, consider the following:

- Short and sweet is best. Do not ramble or post big blocks of type.

- Make your point quickly. Don't make readers go through an entire paragraph or two before they discover your "thesis statement" or lead sentence.

- Start with a common question: "Ever wonder why...?" "How many times have you...?" "Is it just me, or...?" Don't overuse this device, but it can really draw people in when you ask a question they can relate to. Make sure you answer your own question, though, or people will feel cheated.

- Provide useful, helpful advice. Make your readers feel that they will learn something new and fascinating each time they visit your blog.

- Use stories to make your point. The best-selling book in the world (the Bible) is full of parables. There's a reason for that—stories help people understand and remember.

■ Spell check and look for typos. Although people are much more forgiving of mistakes online and in e-mail than they are in print, it's still best to present yourself as a thorough and accurate professional.

■ Be conversational. Write as if you're talking to your best friend. The blog is not a stiff high school English essay, but should feel more like a little chat.

■ Write in first person, using a lot of "I"s and "you"s.

■ Leave 'em hanging. "But that's a whole 'nother story I'll get to next time I write." Tease people into coming back.

■ People love lists. Note that you're reading one right now. They're concise, easy to follow, and easier to remember—your reader may not recall every point, but will have a reason to return to your blog to get everything down. Top Ten lists and Ten Worst lists always get attention.

■ Offer your own unique opinions, but don't be too snarky or critical. Looking at entertainment blogs like Perez Hilton and TMZ you get the feeling that cattiness is in, but you don't want any potential employers to rule you out because they're afraid of your attitude. Witty and positive works much better than sarcastic and negative.

■ Be current and topical. If there's an upcoming political, sports, or entertainment event, like elections, the Super Bowl, or the Oscars, find a way to relate them to your particular topic. Holidays are always fun to weave in as well.

■ A JPG is worth a thousand words. Post as many relevant pictures as you possibly can, and don't even think of creating a site that doesn't have your own picture on it. Avoid photos that are too personal, however, like you unwrapping presents or doing tequila shots with the girls. See a list of sites on page 123 where you can get wonderful free photos in the public domain, which means you don't have to pay for or get permission to use them.

■ Think about embedding video. YouTube and other such sites make this far easier than you might think. You don't have to have exceptional editing skills or an enormous amount of expensive bandwidth to embed video, since you're not actually hosting it on your site. When creating your site, leave a space to embed video, then search the Web for short pieces you think are pertinent or amusing. This will make your site infinitely more interesting and inviting.

■ If you have time to closely monitor your site and you have viewers who would like to chime in, provide a space for comments. Otherwise, disable and hide the "comments" area that almost all sites come with. If it says "0 comments" under each post, it looks like few people ever visit and/or are provoked by your blog. That might be true, but you don't need to advertise it.

■ If you do allow comments, never argue with those who write controversial posts, or try to e-mail them to correct them, contradict them, or explain yourself. There are a lot of nasty people out there who spend most of their time posting critical comments on other people's sites. You will never win an argument with these people, so don't even try. That's another reason why I'm reluctant to allow anyone to post comments on my blog, even if comments help drive loyalty and traffic. When I placed some of my celebrity interviews on YouTube, I had to spend a good deal of time deleting the obscene and otherwise defamatory posts some viewers insisted on writing.

■ Blog as often as you possibly can. Don't let an entire week go by without adding something. I'm always surprised to see blog sites that haven't been added to in several months. What's the point of the blog if you're not going to keep it current? Besides, if people really like your blog, they'll enable an RSS feed that will alert them anytime you post something new. You want to keep them coming back for more.

■ Never write excuses for not blogging often enough. You might not have the time, but you don't want to advertise it. Excuses and apologies are boring and common.

■ Provide helpful links. Ideally, those you link to will link back to you. It's good to have people consider your site a useful resource, and linking makes you more findable and drives traffic to your site.

■ Make your URL part of your brand. Print it on your business cards, and include it in your e-mail signature and on all mentions on social networking sites.

■ If it's important to you to have lots of traffic, you're going to have to learn about SEO (search engine optimization) and SEM (search engine marketing). I posted LisaLiveInHollywood.com as a shamelessly self-promotional website and never planned to carry advertising, so traffic numbers didn't matter to me. But if you're trying to make a little money from your blog and drive traffic to your site, you'll need to brush up in these areas.

ADVICE

SOMETHING FOR NOTHING

There *is* such a thing as a free lunch! (Or at least free photos of it.) Here is a list of free stock-image sites for you to use to brighten up your blog site. Make sure you review the "terms of use" on each site, however, as some have specifications such as "for noncommercial use only."

amygdela.com	photogen.com
burningwell.com	Public-domain-photos.com
dreamstime.com	sxc.hu
energy.star29.net	UnProfound.com
FreeFoto.com	zurb.net
FreeJPG.com	

Bucks for Blogging

It is indeed possible, although very difficult, to make money from your blog. The competition is steep—Technorati.com, a search engine for blogs that tracks popularity and currency, published an article recently that said there are 900,000 new blog posts every day, and that number is growing. Still, Technorati also says there are at least 188.9 million blog posts *read* every day, including posts on Facebook and MySpace, so there are a lot of people out there looking for something to read. Some experts speculate that if you can "just" get 100,000 or more unique visitors a month to your site, you can actually earn an average of around $75,000 annually from click-through advertising and other sources. Click-through ads involve allowing a company like Google to place ads on your site, and earning a certain amount of money each time a viewer clicks through to the advertiser's site from the ad on yours.

Once you carve out a niche for yourself by developing your brand, voice, and traffic, you might be able to join a blog ad network, which bundles blogs according to subject and sells space on them to advertisers. For example, Blogads.com has groups like Lawyers, Economists, Foodies, and so on, and if your blog meets their requirements, they'll take care of selling and placing the advertising and send you a check. It isn't common, but there are people who have made over $100,000 per month using Internet blog advertising services. And while most advertisers are slashing their ad budgets, they seem to be cutting what little they have left from television, radio, magazines, and newspapers and adding it to their Internet advertising budgets.

The "Mommy Blog" Dooce.com is a perfect example of the right content, the right branding, and the right voice at the right time. Blogger Heather Armstrong was going more for personal expression, but her humorous ways of describing her domestic adventures caught on so well that domestic users flocked to her site by the hundreds of thousands, and both she and her husband were able to quit their day jobs. Now Heather blogs full-time, with big-name advertisers like Best Buy, Intel, Spiegel, and Crate and Barrel all on board. But don't quit *your* day job and start blogging just yet. Dooce has about 850,000 viewers.

Making money is all about traffic, my friends. The more traffic, the more money. Some estimates show that advertisers spend the lion's share of their budgets on female-oriented websites, which are seen by upwards of 85 million visitors per month. Going for a piece of that pie is tempting. Wouldn't it be nice if the blog site you develop to get a new job actually *becomes* your new job? I'm just saying...

One way to get instant exposure for your blog and increase the chances of an employer finding you would be to approach an established blog site and offer to post for pay. If you think your blog is so well-written, cutting-edge, insightful, amusing, or whatever, why not approach the major information sites in your field and ask them if they would be willing to work something out? At the very least, they might offer you a "rev share," which involves splitting the profits from the advertising dollars your blog brings in. If their site is bigger, better promoted, and gets more traffic than yours, what have you got to lose?

What Once Was Lost, Now Is Found

Whether you're posting your blog on an already established site or going it on your own, potential employers are more likely to find you if you follow any or all of these suggestions:

■ Use a domain name that contains words that most people search for in your profession, such as PhabulousPharmaceuticalSales.com or RetailManagerMania.com. Go to a site like GoDaddy.com, Network Solutions.com, or WebHosting.yahoo.com and reserve all domain names that are close to the one you've chosen. You can direct traffic to the right one from the others, and they can be as inexpensive as $5 each for a year.

■ Update your blog frequently and use plenty of words that are specific to your industry, so the "bots" that search the Internet for key words will find them and tell the search engines to list your blog closer to the top of a search list that comes up when someone types in those words.

■ Encourage people to quote you on their own websites, use your information, and give you credit for it and provide a link to yours. People who do this are not sponging off you, they're giving you more exposure. Not only will your name get out there, but the more links to your site, the higher you'll score in search engines (that is, when someone does a Google search on your subject, your website will move closer to the beginning of the results list).

■ Establish your identity on other people's blogs. Comment frequently on several of your favorites. This will bring attention and traffic to yours.

■ Post as much "rich," visually interesting content as possible, such as videos and pictures. They're attractive and keep people coming back.

■ Get as many people as you possibly can to link to your site, including your friends with their own blogs or MySpace and Facebook pages. Offer to link to their sites in exchange.

■ Make it so that subscribers can be easily notified each time you post something new. Without getting too technical, it involves something called RSS, and your friendly neighborhood techie, or the sixteen-year-old next door, can probably help you with this.

■ Issue a search-optimized press release—that's a press release with links embedded in it. If your announcement is new and cool enough, all sorts of sites will pick it up and run links to your blog. See Google's "search-optimized press release" to get the most current info on this.

There are many books and experts out there that can help you with your blog or website. One resource I particularly like is Chris Brogan, whose advice and expertise can be found for free on his website, ChrisBrogan.com. He breaks down the most complicated issues so that even the greenest rookie can understand the information quickly and completely, he's willing to answer your questions, and he has a must-read newsletter. Problogger.net also has some good, very basic information, and Daniel Scocco's DailyBlogTips.com is also terrific.

Lisa's ADVICE

YOU'VE GOT TO GIVE A LITTLE

A great way to call a lot more attention to yourself, your skills, and your web/blog site is by leaving comments or participating in discussions on other people's sites. Establish yourself as *the* expert on the topic of your choice, and people will look forward to your posts and search the Web to find more about you. Make sure your comments are helpful and insightful, however, rather than just plain rude or snarky. The Web is full of armchair critics who live to post what they think are clever, derogatory comments about anything and everything. It's best not to criticize too severely, lest your posts be deleted—or, worse, you could find yourself in a pissing match with another poster.

An example of this is a friend who is a C-list media personality, who when she first started out used to post what she considered to be clever retorts to anyone who wrote anything negative on her website. It's a perfectly natural inclination to want to defend yourself, but as you can imagine, these exchanges rapidly degraded into childish tit-for-tats that she answered carelessly in angry haste. They ended up making her look worse than her attacker, and her childish typos and venom landed squarely on Page Six, embarrassing her and anyone associated with her. If you have loyal followers, they will do the defending for you. It's far better to establish your own credibility by participating in positive online discussions and posting good-natured, helpful comments. It's not beyond the realm of possibility to receive job offers or freelance work from others who are in on the discussion with you. I know I've hired writers and researchers this way.

Some Success Stories to Get You Going

I consider myself sort of an "Everywoman," so my own blogging success story might encourage and inspire you. I had the most outrageous good fortune with LisaLiveInHollywood.com less than *three months* after I launched it. I didn't even have time to optimize the site with advertising, affiliate programs, or multiple links. I'd just gotten the bare bones up and running and figured out how to post when an Internet acquisition firm offered to buy my site outright, add it to a site they intended to build, and hire me to run the new site for them full-time. They paid me several times what it cost me to develop and post the site, although it didn't even have any significant traffic yet. The firm didn't care—they were looking for content for a database, and an established journalist with Hollywood connections to create new content for them on a daily basis. Who says you can't have the same kind of luck with your new blog?

I consider Arianna Huffington to be a sort of superwoman, and most of us would be content with a mere fraction of her success, so I think her story will be inspiring and encouraging to you as well. As recently as two years before the last presidential election when Arianna's blog was just beginning, many people thought that "HuffPo" might be some type of breakfast cereal. But the ubiquitous Arianna would soon be leading the top political destination on the Web. The liberal-leaning HuffingtonPost.com had record traffic during the last presidential election year, and is currently worth an estimated $200 million! It utilizes both unpaid bloggers and full-time reporters and editors, and helped pave the way for other popular (female-run) news/blog sites like Wowowow and The Daily Beast. *The Huffington Post Complete Guide to Blogging* is the definitive book on the subject. Go Arianna!

If you really want your blog and/or your career to take off in a big way, it's time to step up your networking game. If you're making a career comeback, chances are the networking scene has been completely redefined since you were last involved with it. But don't fret yet—the next chapter will throw you right in and teach you to swim with the sharks in a few days. You *will* make connections, you *will* be heard, and you *will* get the perfect job—with a little help from your friends.

7

Make the Social Net *Work*

Poverty, I realized, wasn't only a lack of financial
resources; it was isolation from the kind of people that
could help you make more of yourself.
                    —*Keith Ferrazzi,* Never Eat Alone

What's the first thing that comes to mind when you hear the term "social networking"? Getting together with the girls for lunch or drinks? Attending business seminars and trade shows and handing out cards? Watching your kids text their friends all through dinner? You're getting warmer, but you still haven't quite nailed it yet. These days, social networking puts the emphasis on the "net," and refers to making contact and communicating electronically, mostly via the Internet. It involves sites such as MySpace, YouTube, and Facebook, but there is more, so much more, and it is an absolutely essential tool for finding the job you've always wanted. Think of social networking as your new BFF.

When the concept first started, it was mostly the bastion of the eighteen to thirty-four crowd, but it's not just for kids anymore. It's estimated that 46 percent of all women in the United States have used social networking sites, and four out of every ten women in their forties have a profile posted somewhere online, on sites such as MySpace, Facebook, LinkedIn, or Plaxo. Media Metrix reports that there are more female Internet users in the forty-five to fifty-four age category than there are male users of the same age. Some of us use social networking sites to see what our kids are up to or to read and write product reviews and give feedback, but many of us are also using social networks to find jobs for ourselves or to locate candidates for positions we're trying to fill at our own companies. If you're not using these fast and easy employment tools, you're missing out on some incomparable and invaluable opportunities. And the good news is that most of them are *free*! They do, however, require a small investment of time.

When I first became aware of social networking sites several years ago, I remember looking at my nieces' MySpace pages and thinking, "How cute! What a great way to share all those prom pictures and the fun they had on Grad Night at Disneyland!" I saw no place for me in it, however, since I was a little old for proms and didn't know anyone who would be interested in looking at photos of me mugging with my girlfriends. Still, I reluctantly signed up for a Facebook profile page in order to check out a college student one of my nieces was interested in. (Yes, I'm a nosey aunt, but since I have no children of my own, I need some outlet for my protective, maternal instincts.) No sooner had I posted those lovely professional photos I'd had taken and written a little about myself than I began to get messages from people I knew all over the country—distant relatives, friends and former colleagues I hadn't seen in years, even old boyfriends who were now interested in professional connections. Via Facebook, I was able to get and give very welcome and frequent updates. I don't have time to call or e-mail all my friends and colleagues every week, but I grew to love posting and receiving updates and photos that I could view at my leisure. In addition, sharing experiences with my online circle of friends made me feel much more connected. I find it extremely fascinating, not to mention useful, to see a more personal side of the many colleagues I generally see in a professional context.

Fun Facts

FUN FACETS OF FACEBOOK

If you feel like you're aging fast, check out the trends on Facebook. Although women aged fifty-five and over currently make up only about 3 percent of its total users, they're also the fastest-growing U.S. demographic on the site. Over a four-month period recently, their numbers grew 175 percent, and the number of women over fifty-five on Facebook is almost double the number of men the same age. The average Facebook user is also maturing, with about 34 percent of U.S. members aged between thirty-five and forty-nine, and more than 45 percent over twenty-six years old. It couldn't have made better sense, then, for Barbie to get her own Facebook page when she turned fifty in 2009. Barbie, after all, has always been the ultimate hipster.

FYI, Facebook can also make you feel like the ultimate hipster. Recently, a random twenty-four-year-old kid in Utah sent me a message on Facebook—"faced me," if you will—asking me what I was up to and wondering if I was doing anything fun that weekend. He'd apparently seen my photo and nothing more on some mutual acquaintance's friend list. "I'm taking my fifty-year-old self to the Grammys!" I responded. I can only imagine how he felt, but I knew I felt like a million!

Facebook was just the tip of the iceberg. I also posted career profiles on Plaxo.com and LinkedIn.com. My social networking soon began to pay off professionally. Out of the blue, when layoffs were increasing by historic proportions, print publications were slashing their staffs, and my colleagues were losing jobs in droves, I received a surprising call from a headhunter in New York. It seems a glossy, upscale Los Angeles magazine was in need of a new editor in chief. The headhunter had found my name, contact information, and qualifications on LinkedIn .com, and wanted to know if I'd be available for an interview in two weeks, when their representative from New York would be in town. Of course I said yes. Soon after that, an old friend contacted me about hosting, producing, and writing an entertainment show for a cable network where he'd been working.

Now, keep in mind that at the time I was already working as the managing editor for a film website, as an entertainment reporter for sixteen radio stations, and was putting the finishing touches on two

different books for major publishers. I certainly wasn't actively seeking another gig. But another gig was actively seeking me! If I can get
offers via social and professional networking sites when I'm not even
trying, imagine how well you can do if you put a little effort into it.
Social and professional networking sites are amazing tools available to
anyone with computer access, and to think they didn't even exist five
years ago!

As a matter of fact, there are all sorts of classes, workshops, and
articles circulating that teach recruiters and human resources experts
how to better utilize social networking sites to cast the widest nets
and find the best possible job candidates. They're advised to search
LinkedIn and Facebook like there's no tomorrow, to read as many
industry-specific blogs and subscribe to as many online newsletters as
possible, and to follow vocal industry leaders on Twitter. So having a
profile on premier online social networks not only makes it possible for
your best friend from third grade to find you, it makes it possible for
your next fabulous employer to track you down and offer you the job
of your dreams.

Bonnie Laufer Krebs, a Canadian multimedia producer in her forties, started using MySpace and Facebook for personal reasons: as a
way to find old friends from summer camp and to keep track of family
living overseas. But she soon found that the social networking sites
had professional advantages. Not only could she promote and post her
interviews and critiques, but she was able to have direct contact with
her clients themselves and not just their representatives. The sites also
gave her invaluable professional exposure. She was a little concerned,
at first, that her two teenage boys might be embarrassed when their
friends saw their mom on MySpace, but they got over it. "It doesn't
really bother them that much," she says. "They know I'm going to be
checking up on them anyway. What good parent wouldn't? We have
so few friends in common that no one really pays attention to the fact
that their mom is on MySpace." Bonnie suggests resisting the urge to
post messages on your kids' pages and to concentrate on your own. She
says it's a little like shopping in separate departments in a large store,
and checking in with each other every now and then. Your teenagers'
friends don't have to know that Mom is in the house.

At the time of publication, the top social/professional networking sites included MySpace, Facebook, Plaxo, LinkedIn, and Twitter, with Facebook and LinkedIn being the sites professionals found most useful. Each has its advantages and unique purposes.

MySpace. It might sound strange to call something born in 2003 the "granddaddy" of all social networking sites still in existence, but MySpace gets that honor. In 2005 MySpace was purchased by Rupert Murdoch's News Corp. for about $327 million, which just goes to show you the value of an idea whose time has come. A few years ago anyone who was anyone under the age of thirty had a MySpace page, but in August 2008 Facebook overtook it in terms of international popularity. Still, MySpace attracts upwards of 230,000 new users per day. There are literally hundreds of millions of MySpace accounts, making it an amazing resource for launching new products and for little-known musicians of all ages to get their music heard. So if your new career involves creating new music or selling a product or service online, MySpace is an incredible resource. It's also a very useful tool for self-promotion.

Facebook. This, the most popular of all free-access networking sites, began as a way for Harvard students to get to know each other, then expanded to other universities, and is now worldwide, for all ages. It's so popular that some companies ban access to it in the workplace, because it's just too darn distracting and engrossing. Many of the original college student users are annoyed that the rest of the world has discovered Facebook and made it a vital networking site for everyone, but they'll just have to get used to the fact that millions of people make professional and social contact via Facebook on a daily basis. There were more than 200 million users worldwide when this book went to press, and I'm sure the numbers have grown considerably since then. Many employers search the site for appropriate job candidates. As a matter of fact, a free Facebook page can substitute for a blog or website if your resources are limited.

Plaxo. It began as an online address book service, but quickly grew into a professional networking site. At last count before publication it had more than 20 million users, and it was growing daily. It's known as sort of a digital, online Rolodex, and the information you store on it can be kept private or shared. You can invite your friends, family, and colleagues to join, giving you access to their most recent contact information without having to call them up and write it down. Another useful networking feature is the weekly e-mail updates you can sign up for, letting you know when people in your network make new connections, or when others with whom you might have something in common join. Although Plaxo is a very useful tool in making business contacts, many users say its best function is as a contact information repository, and do the majority of their business networking on LinkedIn.com.

LinkedIn. At last count it boasted more than 38 million members, and adds new ones at a rate of 1.2 million per month, which boils down to about one new user every two seconds. It's definitely more of an executive-level networking site—you won't find too many angst-ridden teens sharing information about their favorite bands here. In fact, the average age of LinkedIn users is forty-one and they have an income of over $51,000. More than 60 percent of LinkedIn users have executive-level or successful consultant positions. On LinkedIn, you will find résumés and recommendations of top-tier executives, as well as those just getting their start in virtually every industry. Major politicians like Barack Obama and Hillary Clinton posted profile pages during the elections, and most heads of major corporations are listed there. Not only is it useful for keeping track of updated contact information for business professionals in your field, but it's a way for you to personally reach out to employers. If you know someone who knows someone who works for a company where you're interested in working, you can ask for an introduction. LinkedIn, when used correctly, can serve as private, backdoor access to the people and businesses you really want to approach.

Twitter. Twitter is a micro-blogging and social networking site that enables users to create messages limited to 140 characters and post them for their followers to receive online, via text message, or in the form of an instant message. The site defines itself as "a service for friends, family, and co-workers to communicate and stay connected through the exchange of quick, frequent answers to one simple question: **What are you doing?**" Individual messages are called "tweets" and users utilize them to keep up with friends, as well as to track the most up-to-the-minute trends, political happenings, even sales and product arrivals at their favorite stores. You've heard that stars like Ashton Kutcher, Demi Moore, and Oprah are tweeting, and it seems that more are joining their ranks every hour. While some people, particularly those over forty, believe that tweets are just too much information to deal with, many people are adapting them as a way to keep on top of a multitude of situations all at once, and as a way to promote themselves, their products, and their services.

How Social Networking Helped Build a Brilliant Business and Create Jobs for Others

The glorious thing about online social networking is that, in addition to your being able to reach out to others, others can reach out to you. Anna Barber, a mother and entrepreneur with a law degree from Yale, said she couldn't have started her brilliant new business without social networking. She used it to secure financing, materials, expertise, retail space, and employees. Her story shows true genius and can be an inspiration to us all.

The business she started is one of those that makes you smack yourself in the forehead and cry, "Of course! Why didn't I think of that?" In a nutshell, she describes it as "Build-a-Bear for books." You and your child can walk into her Scribble Press facility in the Westside Pavilion in Los Angeles and emerge a couple hours later with a beautiful, professionally bound book, written and illustrated by your child. There are myriad art and printing materials, multiple book formats, and birthday party facilities in her colorful venue, and art classes for children of all ages are held there each week. As children's bedrooms fill up and start overflowing with hand-decorated and dressed stuffed toys, parents feel they can never have too many original, customized books, and they make priceless, one-of-a-kind gifts for others. I'm thinking Scribble Press will go nationwide in a matter of seconds.

Anna and her partner Darcy Pollack, who holds an MBA from Harvard and is also a mother in her forties, met one day on a plane, immediately bonded, and freely admit they'd never have been able to start their dream business without the Internet. "We were able to find all the supplies and equipment we needed, plus specialists in this field, on the Internet," they enthuse. They advise everyone to embrace the technology available. "We all really need to be out there on LinkedIn, Facebook, and Twitter," says Anna. "They are powerful tools for staying relevant. When I graduated from law school in 1995, few people had cell phones or were using the Internet." No one knows better than Anna how quickly times change, and how important it is to use the tools available to keep up with them—even if you're in a quaintly old-fashioned industry like bookbinding.

Social Networking Power Tools

Just as a hammer and a screwdriver are probably the most useful implements in a toolbox, I'm going to go out on a limb here and state that Facebook and LinkedIn are probably the most useful sites in your online career networking tool kit. There are millions of professionals, including Anna Barber, who agree with me. I would suggest getting involved with all the career networking sites that pertain to your field, but if you concentrate on these two, you won't regret the time and effort spent. And by the way, expense is not an issue. Their free services are superb, although enhanced features and services can be purchased at reasonable prices. I've done extensive research and conducted many interviews about these two sites to come up with the following tips for using them to your maximum advantage:

Linking Up with LinkedIn in Three Easy Steps

If you're at all active on the Internet, you've probably received invitations from friends or acquaintances to join their LinkedIn network.

You might have visited the site and filled in rudimentary information such as contact info and a little bit about yourself professionally. As you look for a new job or for more opportunities in your current company, you'll want to start taking advantage of everything this networking site has to offer. This can be done quickly and easily.

1. Join LinkedIn and complete your profile. If you haven't done this already, be sure to fill out the requested profile information. The more thoroughly you complete your profile, the better chance potential employers will have of finding you. It's very simple, and involves little more than filling in the blanks. You can cut and paste blocks of copy from your résumé if you like. Plus, it's one more place to post those gorgeous photos you've had taken.

2. Start connecting. I'll be happy to be your first connection, but LinkedIn will automatically supply you with the names of people you might know from past jobs or the educational institutions you've attended, as listed in your profile. If there are savvy professionals whom you know as friends, business acquaintances, people you've worked with on committees, or at church, chances are they're on LinkedIn too. Do a search for them, and request a connection. Use your yearbooks and old directories from companies or organizations to find names you might have forgotten. You can also upload your Internet contact list, and if any of the names in your file are on LinkedIn, you should request connections with them. Don't worry about them thinking that you're pestering them or, worse, trying to use or take advantage of them. Who knows? They might be considering asking you for help. Most people on LinkedIn realize it's a mutually beneficial service.

3. Write and request recommendations. When you find colleagues whom you respect and know well enough, ask them to write a recommendation for you, and offer to do the same for them. Potential employers definitely take time to read the recommendations posted on your LinkedIn profile, and they carry a lot of weight. You can choose to post or omit the recommendations others write for you if you don't particularly like the way they sound.

These steps are just the basics to start you off and get you noticed for jobs immediately. If you'd like to utilize LinkedIn further, there are all sorts of cool tools to use, including joining various groups on the site that pertain to your particular profession, school, interests, or political beliefs. You can also take advantage of site applications that allow you to post slideshow presentations and videos, create your own blog, and to upload large files.

This is hardly the definitive guide to making the most of LinkedIn. You'll find any of the following books to be very helpful:

1. *I'm on LinkedIn, Now What???: A Guide to Getting the Most Out of LinkedIn*, by Jason Alba, Happy About Press. Despite its inappropriate use of three question marks in the title, this book is a useful guide for the beginner.

2. *LinkedIn for Dummies*, by Joel Elad, For Dummies. I'm a big fan of the For Dummies series because it boils everything down for the most low-tech neophyte, and doles out information in easy-to-digest bites.

3. *Let's Connect: Using LinkedIn to Get Ahead at Work*, by Ajay Jain, TCP Media Private Limited. This book is very instructional, with Jain giving examples of how many people have used LinkedIn to their professional advantage.

Finding Face Time on Facebook in Three Easy Steps

Facebook is a more social site than LinkedIn, which is almost exclusively professional. Still, don't rule out the infinite professional possibilities Facebook has to offer. The network gives you the opportunity to present a more well-rounded, up-to-the minute picture of yourself, and even show off a little of your sense of humor. Here's how it works:

1. **Sign up for a Facebook page.** Use three names, first, middle, and last, or, if you're married, use your maiden name and your married

name—it will be easier for people to find you. For example, if your name is Karen Reid, a search will reveal hundreds of Karen Reids. But if your maiden name is Madsen and you sign up as Karen Madsen Reid, there will be no mistaking you for someone else. Now fill in as much or as little personal information as you see fit. There are spaces for you to put your favorite TV shows, music, movies, books, activities, interests, even your favorite questions, but all that is not necessary, and perhaps even undesirable. You want people to believe you have a real, busy life outside of Facebook, and might not have the time or desire to share every detail of your personal life. Do, however, go into detail on the Education and Work sections. Use the fabulous photo you had taken for your main profile shot. Whatever you do, if you're going to use this for professional purposes, don't make the first photo people see of you a picture of your pets, your children, or your second-grade school photo. Also, as you post more photos, avoid those of you doing tequila shots in Cancun. They will come back to bite you in the butt. Just ask anyone who's ever been on a *Girls Gone Wild* video.

2. Start searching for friends. Begin with the names of close friends and family, because they're easy. Again, I'll be happy to be your friend if you send me a little message telling me you read this book. Once people start "accepting" you as a friend, you'll have access to their lists of friends, and you should go through them to see if any mutual acquaintances are listed. Feel free to reach out to them and invite them to be your friend. Before you know it, people from your past will be contacting you to be their friends. During my first months on Facebook, I found it fabulous to reconnect with friends, relatives, and business associates I hadn't heard from in years. You can also find friends and gain exposure by joining various groups. You'll find fan groups of everyone from Jesus Christ to Inigo Montoya on Facebook.

3. Post away! Frequently (at least two to three times per week) post updates on your own wall, and make comments on your friends' walls. Beware of what you post, however. Mundane postings like "Lisa is happy" or "Lisa is home from work" will cause people to ignore you. If I were to write messages like "Lisa is going to bed now" on my wall, people would start snoring right along with me. But friends love to read about amusing, ironic, or bizarre things that happen to you, and your original or radical opinions are always fun to read. Because I'm an author and film critic, I also like to post (short) opinions of books I've read or films I've seen. When I hear something that surprises or delights me, I post that. In turn, when someone else posts something surprising or delightful, I comment on it. The more you write clever things on other people's walls, the more exposure you get. If you recently got laid off and/or are looking for work, comment on your own search, and ask others for their advice and opinions. You never know: One of your friends might have a friend who has a friend who can help you out.

Facebook also has a Marketplace where you can look for jobs in your field and post an ad about what you're looking for. Or you can create a page for your business, which is a good idea even if you have your own blog or website. In addition, there are tools to help you connect your Facebook profile to LinkedIn and other networking sites.

For more information on how to make the most of Facebook, I recommend any of the following publications:

1. *Facebook: The Missing Manual*, by E. A. Vander Veer, Pogue Press. Explaining how to get maximum benefit from Facebook for professional and personal purposes, this illustrated publication gives essential etiquette tips and shows you how to use applications.

2. *Facebook for Dummies*, by Carolyn Abram and Leah Pearlman, For Dummies. Again, the For Dummies books are always thorough, easy reads. This one shows you how to use the site to network and market like a veteran.

3. *I'm on Facebook, Now What???: How to Get Personal, Business, and Professional Value from Facebook*, by Jason Alba and Jesse Stay, Happy About Press. As you already know, all those question marks really bug me, but they don't distract from the clear, concise information contained in this book.

To Tweet or Not to Tweet

As mentioned previously, Twitter is an instant micro-blog service through which you can send mini-texts or instant messages to many people at the same time. You can write your own "tweets" and hope someone follows you, and/or you can follow other people and it's all free. The Twitter.com website explains it all:

> Why? Because even basic updates are meaningful to family members, friends, or colleagues—especially when they're timely.
>
> **Eating soup?** Research shows that moms want to know.
>
> **Running late to a meeting?** Your co-workers might find that useful.
>
> **Partying?** Your friends may want to join you.

Twitter is not just for kids, either. Legitimate news services like CNN, Newswise, and the *New York Times* will send you the latest headlines via Twitter, then you can log on to their websites to get the rest of the story if it's important to you. When the commercial jet landed on the Hudson, people on the West Coast heard about it before the plane even came to a stop, because their New York friends were tweeting about it. It's a dream come true if you're an extreme news junkie. You'll always be the best-informed and most up-to-the-minute person in the room. Many people also use Twitter as a great way to make professional contacts. Say a magazine writer sends out a tweet calling for insight on a certain subject that happens to be your specialty. You tweet a response, she calls you and requests an interview. Voilà! You have exposure as an expert that you never would have had without Twitter, and if she ends up quoting you, your professional brand gets amazing exposure.

If your head starts spinning when you contemplate receiving and reading mini-messages at all hours of the day and night, Denise E. Zimmerman, the fortysomething president and CSO of NetPlus Marketing, Inc., has this to say about the virtues of Twitter: "It's not really about the technology, it's about the people. For professional purposes, it's a way of getting your brand out there, or getting to know other people's brands. Technology today advances your ability to connect with others faster and more efficiently, with further reach than ever before."

She suggests that the less outgoing among us simply follow tweets of people in the industry that interests us, to keep up on trends and advancements. Someone who's in the apparel industry, for example, can follow updates and news from hot designers and fashion bloggers. "Who knows?" she asks. "You might one day find yourself being interviewed by one of these people for a job." They would be extremely impressed if they found out you'd been following them on Twitter.

For those who are passionate and outspoken, Zimmerman suggests tweeting about your field of interest and acquiring a following. "It's a great way to establish your own personal brand," she says. "The exciting thing about Twitter," Zimmerman adds, "is that you are free to define it for yourself. Once you get a feel for it, you can figure out how to make it work for you. There's no risk involved," she points out. She's right. You can't get hurt or lose money with Twitter (unless you accidentally post really embarrassing personal information, which is not easy to do: "Whoops! I just typed in my darkest secret and sent it to all my followers! How did that happen?"). Zimmerman suggests starting out by looking her up and sending her a tweet. She can be reached at http://Twitter.com/DZimmerman.

Lisa's ADVICE

HOW I USE TWITTER

I'd heard a lot about how narcissistic Twitter can be. I mean, really, who cares if I'm ducking into the Starbucks on Robertson and Beverly for a latte? Although many people give location updates in hopes of having their friends join them, I don't use it that way. I use Twitter to give people blog entry updates when I write about subjects I think might be of use to them—tweets like "Find out how to laugh off a layoff" and "Make your layoff pay off." Those kinds of tweets help the people who read them and bring traffic to my site.

A FUN, PROFESSIONAL NETWORKING EXERCISE

Maybe you're a little shy or not too savvy when it comes to online networking. Here is a fun and easy way to get started. Even if you're at the top of your LinkedIn game, this exercise could be a new and exciting way to get access to the job you really want. Be aware that the majority of job openings are not posted either online or in the paper, and many jobs are posted in-house first, giving employees a chance to fill them themselves, or with their colleagues or friends who come highly recommended. So I suggest you try a specific "Employer Search," rather than a job search. It's simple and can be great fun. It's an easy, three-step process:

1. Identify a company that you would like to work for. Let's say you've always wanted to be a Disney employee (although hopefully you've gotten past that adolescent fantasy of wanting to be Mulan in the Main Street Parade). Type "Disney" into whatever social network you belong to; I'd suggest trying LinkedIn first. You will automatically receive a long list of people who have the word "Disney" in their profiles. LinkedIn will let you know how many degrees of separation there are between you and those people, and if you have any friends in common.

2. Select the right contacts. Take note of the people who appear to be in the department where you'd like to work. Do you know any of them or have a personal connection? If not, take those names and type them, one at a time, into your favorite search engine. Find out as much *professional* information about them as you can. They might have a blog, or have been quoted in a newspaper article. These are good details to have when you contact them.

3. Make contact. If your search on LinkedIn reveals that you have a mutual friend, ask that friend to recommend you and make an online introduction. If you have no connections whatsoever, you can still send them a message through the site and they can decide whether or not they want to answer and connect. Whatever you do, however, don't state that you're looking for a job in your first message. Establish professional rapport with them first. This is where the research comes in. Write something like, "I read in the *Times* that you just got promoted. I'm in the same field, and know how challenging it can be. Congratulations!" Or, "I noted that your company is investing in green renovations, and would like to know a little more." Or, best of all, "I have a blog on marketing, and wanted to quote you, since you seem to be the expert." The old "I'd like to quote you on my blog" works best because you can send them your URL and they'll get to know you immediately. After you've been accepted as a contact or a friend and established rapport, *then* and *only then* can you ask about any job openings they might have. Chances are they receive—and reject—direct job inquiries all the time. It's best to finesse them a little first.

TO MAKE EVEN MORE CONNECTIONS

Facebook and LinkedIn are just the beginning. There are countless secondary professional networking sites, many being industry-specific. The following is a list of websites that might be helpful to you in your efforts to reach out and connect with others in your field and find jobs there:

AlumWire.com. For those interested in university-level education, this is a platform that bridges the gap between alumni networks and recruiters through résumé collections, job postings, and chat booth technology.

ArtBreak.com. A site for the artistic among us to share and sell their work.

Blogtronix.com. An "Enterprise Social Platform" with a suite of tools including blogs, wikis, documents, and social media.

BooksConnect.com. If you're in a literary field or the publishing industry, this is a great, easy-to-navigate site that connects readers, authors, publishers, librarians, and booksellers.

Brightfuse.com. Launched by CareerBuilder.com, it's an uncomplicated yet extensive site for professional networking.

Change.org. A fabulous, nonprofit social networking site that asks what you want to change in the world, connects you with like-minded folks, and provides opportunities for work or volunteerism.

Classmates.com. More than just a social site that connects you with former schoolmates, many people use this for professional networking as well. It seems that some people are more willing to help out their favorite classmates, whom they've known and trusted for years.

Decorati.com. A global resource where those interested in interior design can shop, learn, connect, and blog.

Dice.com. *The* career community for positions in the information technology industry.

Doostang.com. An invite-only networking site where you can make professional connections via Facebook, your alma mater, your company, and more.

eFinancialCareers.com. Everything you need to know about getting hired in the hard-hit finance industry.

Eons.com. A social and professional networking site geared toward Baby Boomers, mostly fifty-plus. Even if you don't fit into this category, these people could become your bosses or mentors, so it doesn't hurt to connect with them.

FastPitchNetworking.com. A one-stop shop for business professionals to network and market their businesses.

Glassdoor.com. This is a salary-review and employee-review site that gives you a look at over 18,000 companies and includes salaries and ratings as well as reviews, posted anonymously by employees. Here you can find out what people with similar jobs in your area are making.

Greenvoice.com. Connect with others who are environmentally conscious and get ideas for careers, volunteers, green living, and community issues.

ImageKind.com. A community for buying, selling, and creating art.

Jigsaw.com. A free business card networking directory where users can establish contacts and get complete, collaborative business information.

Konnects.com. A place where you can create your own professional networking communities.

MediaBistro.com. An outstanding networking community and job site for those in all aspects of the media business, from print to broadcast to electronic.

MyStore.com. An alternative to eBay and Amazon, this community site allows you to sell your own products and get deals on others. It's one of the simplest seller sites out there.

RealMatch.com. Post your résumé on this site and they'll nofify you when a job opening that fits comes along. A great, less time-consuming alternative to sites like Monster.com and CareerBuilder.com.

Ryze.com. A free site that helps you expand your business network with job contacts, career building, and sales tools.

Spoke.com. Expand your business network internationally via this site that gives you access to more than 40 million people worldwide.

TheLadders.com. A well-known, well-used site for employees seeking jobs that pay more than $100K.

www.usajobs.gov. This is the government's official job site, and will tell you everything you need to know about getting hired by Uncle Sam. There are usually around 50,000 jobs listed here.

Networking the Old-Fashioned Way: Face-to-Face

As fabulous as online social networking can be, however, you don't want to leave out another tried-and-true form of connecting that women have been enjoying for centuries. Ellen Bravo, author of *Taking on the Big Boys: Why Feminism Is Good for Families* and the former director of 9to5, the National Association of Working Women, who now teaches women's studies at the University of Wisconsin–Milwaukee, advises networking the good old-fashioned way: forming a group of like-minded peers. She suggests getting together with other people who are seeking jobs or promotions, and giving and getting feedback. Look over each other's résumés, practice interviewing skills and elevator pitches, pass along leads that could include any job opportunities or openings you hear about. "The best way to get what you need is to work with others on behalf of everyone," says Ellen. She's all about working *with* each other rather than *against* each other. If everyone had that attitude, we'd all be gainfully employed in jobs we love. Now *that's* what I'm talking about.

8

Botox Your Résumé

The secret to staying young is to live honestly, eat slowly, and lie about your age.

—*Lucille Ball*

Your résumé is *supposed* to be an advertisement for your own fresh, professional brand, but mine was showing me off to be about as cool and hip as Betty Crocker. It was that one little line at the beginning, which read, "More than twenty-five years of experience," that was slowing people down. Surely, the young HR professional thinks, someone with that much experience must by now be wearing bifocals and a crocheted shawl, yes?

I was stunned to look at it from that point of view. Whoever dreamed that all that experience could be a liability? How could one little line like that pile on a perceived fifteen pounds, fifteen years, fifteen wrinkles, and more than 15,000 gray hairs? As my husband gently and cautiously attempted to point out, when a prospective employer does the math, he or she figures I graduated when I was twenty-one, adds twenty-five years of experience to that, and you have a forty-six-year-old lady. Some people have quite respectably become grandmothers by the age of forty-six! While Baby Boomers may be healthier, stronger, and more energetic in their forties, fifties, and sixties than any other generation has ever been, when people in their twenties think of people in their forties, they don't conjure up images of Kyra Sedgwick, Sheryl Crow, or Gwen Stefani, they think Martha Stewart, Diane Sawyer, and Helen Mirren, even though those women are in their sixties. Hey, I remember being twenty years old and staring over at my college roommate who was twenty-four and working on her master's, thinking, "She's really getting up there! If I'm still single and in college when I'm her age, I'll shoot myself!" (I obviously didn't. I may have graduated when I was twenty-one, but I didn't get married until I was forty-eight!) Back to the present, regarding my résumé, as my husband so painfully pointed out, "Twenty-five years of experience just makes you look old."

If I was going to compete with Generations X and Y for jobs, I needed a little "Botox for the résumé," a phrase coined for me by the *Wall Street Journal*. To be sure, I needed more than just Botox—my résumé could have used a complete facelift, from neck to crown. So my husband and I got busy with a little computerized scalpel—well, a chain saw is more like it. We trimmed and hacked away at all those years of experience until a vibrant, capable woman of indeterminate age emerged.

Once I started sending out this new, revamped and revitalized résumé, I began receiving responses and requests for interviews within twenty minutes! Just to see if this sudden success was a fluke, I sent this new résumé to the unresponsive companies that had previously received the old résumé, and even they called me back promptly, as if they'd never heard of me before! Some professional résumé-writing companies may pooh-pooh my technique, but you can't argue with success. Within three weeks of sending out the new résumé, I'd received five good offers and accepted two of them. I went from being a free-lancer whose net declared income was about $3,000 (according to my brother-in-law, a very savvy CPA) to a fully disclosed six-figure salary! While there was no getting around that sum with clever deductions, I was absolutely ecstatic to pay taxes on it. All this, plus I now had benefits and stock options? That's what Botoxing, or age-proofing, my résumé did for me, and it can do the same for you.

Now, I'm not saying age-proofing your résumé is easy, and it's not necessarily fun. I fought my husband every year of the way to keep all my experience in there—after all, I'd achieved many a coup, skill, and honor in those first ten or fifteen years of my professional life that we were talking about slicing off, and I was reluctant to cast any of them aside. My magazine articles had been translated into twenty different languages, for heaven's sake. I'd won Sigma Delta Chi awards, and I'd shot photos that graced the covers of magazines! Weren't those accomplishments worth inclusion on my résumé?

Not exactly—not chronologically, anyway. Things have changed considerably in the past twenty-five years, and the technology I'd used then has little application in the workplace today. Those cover shots were taken on Kodachrome, back in the days when you shot and processed twenty or thirty rolls of film in the hope of ending up with two usable photos. The magazine articles that were printed in twenty different languages were processed on a computer housed in its own climatically controlled office that was bigger than my living room, and the magazine pages were laid out with an X-Acto knife and wax.

Think about what you were doing twenty-five years ago. Back then, there was no Internet, there were no survivors on reality TV, and MTV showed music videos. Twenty-five years ago big hair, jumpsuits, and high-topped tennies were the height of fashion. Twenty-five years ago Ronald Reagan was alive and in office and Barack Obama was still in law school at Harvard. Portable phones were the size of bricks, and even the most advanced computers could process about one-millionth of the information they can process today. Since every major industry and field has changed drastically in the last ten years, let alone the last twenty-five, there isn't a lot of experience from "way back when" that would be relevant today. The last thing you want to say in an interview with a potential employer who comments on your past work experience is, "Well, that was a while back. We did things differently then." That makes you sound so old and stale!

My "before" résumé showed me working as an editor at an international teenage magazine. As much fun as I had and as much as I learned at the magazine from October 1985 through May 1994, that job was the first to go. And my three-year stint before that as the managing editor of a special-interest community weekly tabloid was dumped along with it. I lopped off twelve years from my age with a tap and a click of the keyboard. This was way better than Botox or plastic surgery—it didn't even hurt, no anesthesia was required, it was free, and there was no recovery time!

Omitting work experience is perfectly moral and honest. You are not stating false information about where you worked, how long you worked there, or what you learned while you were employed. You are not stating false information at all. The only work experience a potential employer is interested in is the work experience that pertains directly

to the job you're applying for. Think of your résumé as an advertisement, and you are the product. An ad is a brief synopsis of a product's
highlights, not a long list of every single feature.

What to Omit from Your Résumé

While we're on the subject of omitting work experience that dates back
more than fifteen years, here's a list of other items you'll want to consider
leaving out. You may remember reading somewhere that this information
should always be included, but I'll bet that source is at least ten years old.

1. Date of graduation. Your university, major, and degree are
important. If you didn't go to college, the fact that you graduated from
high school is important. Your date of graduation is not. In my case, I
graduated in three years, so my graduation date falsely adds a perceived
extra year to my age.

2. Your birthdate. Don't laugh—a friend of mine showed me her
résumé and she had that right at the top under her name and address.

3. The dates you began and finished certain jobs. I leave this
up to your own discretion. What's really important to convey is the
amount of time you spent on the job, not specifically when you worked
there. Some employers think you're trying to hide something, like a
gap in employment, if you leave them off, however. Other times, dates
can be confusing, such as if you taught at a certain school for a while,
went to another, then returned to the first one. Rather than confuse the
employer, just list the amount of time you taught at each.

4. The phrase, "References available upon request." That's a
waste of time and space. That you are willing to supply references is
taken for granted.

**5. Outdated technology skills or industry-related terminol-
ogy.** Pay attention to ads for jobs in your field to find out what employers

are looking for these days. Get rid of obsolete computer programs that you learned back in the good old days.

6. Your actual street address. It's fine to list the city you live in, but the address of your actual residence is unnecessary. If you have a URL (Web address), use that instead. If potential employers need to mail you something—which is highly unlikely since so many people now communicate digitally—they can ask for your street address. Chances are you'll be submitting your résumé electronically (via the Internet), so it's your e-mail address that is truly important. Who knows what types of biases your street address could bring up? Even if you live in an upscale neighborhood, a recruiter could have been tormented by a bully who comes from your neck of the woods, and subconsciously hold that against you. Also, some employers are looking for someone with a short commute, and you may be perfectly willing to relocate, but that's Too Much Information (TMI) for the résumé. If your address is too posh you might be perceived as not needing the job. If it's not posh enough, you might be perceived as unqualified. This is often subliminal, but people can't help thinking these things. It's best not to be judged in any way by your address.

7. Anything that lengthens your résumé to more than two pages. The old rule that everything should fit on one page no longer applies, but more than two pages implies that you don't stay in any one position very long. Omit the jobs that lasted less than six months to one year if you have to. An acquaintance of mine proudly showed me his résumé recently, which he'd paid hundreds of dollars to have professionally crafted. It was more than five pages long, and included positions he'd held for less than four months. Any employer looking at that would assume he was either restless or got fired a lot. Judging by the amount of anger he displayed when I suggested he cut it back, I'm guessing it was the latter. Whatever the case, the professional résumé company he'd chosen appeared to be more concerned with justifying its large fees and the obscenely long amount of time they took, instead of writing a productive résumé for him.

8. Negative information. Even if the company you worked for went out of business or there were massive layoffs and your dismissal was not your fault, you don't need to include that on your résumé. You will probably be asked about that in your job interview or on your application.

9. Exaggerations or untruths. That little white lie could come back to bite you in the butt. Go on the theory that every detail—and I mean *every* detail—will be substantiated by a fact checker in the human resources department. Why would you want to start a working relationship with lies to cover up anyway?

10. Type smaller than 10-point. Any smaller is difficult for most people to read, and your résumé might be put aside just because it's too much effort.

What to Include on Your Résumé

So now that we've pretty much covered what shouldn't be on your résumé, let's talk about what should be there.

1. Your contact information, right at the top. This should include your full name (no Ms. or Mrs.), your city of residence, your phone number, your e-mail address, and your website or blog address. By the way, if you've been using the same e-mail address forever and it's a cutesy one that doesn't include your real name, I'd get a new one and use it specifically for your job search—so many different sites offer free e-mail addresses, but Gmail (Google) seems to be most in vogue right now. Or use the one that you get free with your website, for example, Margot@MargotChase.com.

2. Career summary. This is a list of your best and brightest accomplishments and skills, and should be featured, with bullets, right under your contact info. It should not be a big block of type in paragraph format.

3. Key words. Take a look at the job descriptions of the positions that interest you and note specific skills and phrases that are used. These are often industry-specific, but include phrases like, "computer savvy," "self-starter," "customer service," etc. Sprinkle these key words liberally throughout your résumé, but don't overuse any one in particular. Sometimes a computer, rather than a human, will be the first to scan your résumé, and if it doesn't see the words or phrases it's programmed to look for, it will automatically discard the résumé.

4. Professional experience or employment history. This is a list of the jobs you've held and a description of them, in reverse chronological order (the most recent first), working backward to anything under fifteen years. In the description of your duties at your previous jobs, make sure you point out accomplishments, achievements, results, etc. For example, "increased sales by 30 percent," "successfully launched new product lines," "increased circulation," etc. Accomplishments and results are even more important than a basic job description. This is where the over-forty worker shines—you probably have more achievements and accomplishments than your younger competition.

5. A list of skills that are related to your field, especially technological skills. These can be included in your job descriptions, if you're short on two-page space.

6. Your education. This should include any degrees and educational honors, plus a list of work-related courses, seminars, workshops, etc., that you've attended. If you haven't attended any, I suggest you do so immediately, to find out what's going on in your field and make contacts. If you attended them many years ago, leave off dates.

7. Interests, activities, and professional memberships. This area sets you apart. If you are a volunteer in any charitable organizations or are a member of any professional organizations, list them here. List any skills, interests, or hobbies that could make you a more valuable employee, or show that you are a positive, energetic, well-rounded person, such as an interest in golf, tennis, historical fiction, public speaking, etc. If you've been active in your church service organization, mention—without disclosing your particular denomination—that you volunteer with organizations helping women in need, or organize meals for the homeless, etc. This is the section employers often choose to begin a live interview conversation, in order for both to establish some simple personal connection. It's also the only place on your résumé where you can share a shred of your sense of humor, if you wish, as I did when I listed, "*dog park devotee*—in the company of our golden doodle pup 'KC.'"

Most Important of All

Print out your résumé and proofread it at least three times. In addition, have someone else—your sister, your mother, your husband, your high school English teacher, any literate person you know—proof it for you. It is imperative that your résumé be perfect. One grammatical error or misspelling can cost you the job.

When I was working as the editor in chief of a magazine in Los Angeles, I actually received an e-mail solicitation from a copyediting company, in response to my ad for a part-time copy editor. The message was *full of typos*! I shouldn't have responded, but I couldn't resist correcting the e-mail and returning it, asking how they expected to get work with an application so riddled with errors. I received an indignant reply accusing me of being a grammar nazi and informing me that they had many satisfied clients. They didn't bother to list them, however, and guess who didn't get the job?

Three Types of Résumés

There are basically three types of résumés used frequently today: the chronological, which lists jobs as you had them, from most recent to farthest in the past; the functional, which you might select if you have big gaps in your employment history or if you have a number of jobs that lasted a short while, and you don't want to specifically describe each one; and the hybrid of the two.

The Chronological Résumé

Chronological résumés are organized by experience and/or jobs, listing the company, your position, a job description, and your accomplishments, in reverse chronological order (most recent job first, then working back). There could be a "Career Objective" statement at the top and a list of accomplishments, followed by a brief career summary. This is probably the most common type, and the one that was suggested to you when you were fresh out of school. The drawback is that it can look stodgy and old-fashioned if you don't add some stylish layout to it.

The Functional Résumé

A functional résumé gives a list of special skills, functions, and/or a summary of career highlights. After that comes a list of employers, with dates omitted. This works well if you are just going back to work and you don't want to emphasize the fact that you haven't had a full-time job in twenty years. It also works well if you haven't had a job in one particular field, but you do have the skills that would make you successful in it. The drawback is that it can be confusing, and employers might correctly assume that you're being coy and trying to hide something.

The Hybrid Résumé

This is the ideal that seems to work best in today's job market. It lists specific skills and career highlights at the top, then goes on to give a brief career history with bulleted mention of the great things accomplished in each position, and the specific talents required. It's eye-catching, easy to read, and shows that you put some actual thought and creativity into the crafting of your résumé, instead of simply going by a dull, standard form.

What follows is a sampling of "before" and "after" résumés, including my own, so you can see how specific tweaks can make a huge difference. In my case, it took me from a four-figure job to a six-figure job in a matter of days.

Before:

Lisa Johnson Mandell
0000 Belford Ave.
Los Angeles, CA 91005
(818) 000-0000
lola1234@earthlink.net

CAREER SUMMARY: Award-winning journalist with 25 years of professional experience in print and broadcast journalism, marketing, and public relations. Developed, produced, and promoted websites, magazines, books, radio shows, and television projects. Skilled in media production of all types and as on-air talent. Managed successful strategic marketing and development projects for profit and nonprofit organizations. Work has been translated into 20 different languages, and is fluent in Spanish.

PROFESSIONAL
EXPERIENCE   **IN HOLLYWOOD PRODUCTIONS**: President
January 2001–present
Produces Internet, television, radio, and print content as well as public relations and marketing materials, including books, magazine articles, scripts, newsletters, television news pieces, and radio programming. Clients have included Comcast, Fox News, Bravo, Greenstone Media, Tribute Entertainment, CitySearch.com, Forbes.com, the *New York Times*, the *Times* of London, Sundance, AP, Random House, St. Martin's Press, CNBC, Paramount Domestic Television, KTLA, Dr. Phil, *Forbes*, Telemundo, Midwest Family Radio, Filmstew.com, the Learning Annex, and many others. Manages freelance specialists and content providers.

SUNDAY LUXURY: Editor in Chief
May 2005–December 2005
Created, marketed, launched, and promoted weekly magazine and corresponding website. Acquired and edited all content. Managed staff of writers, editors, columnists, photographers, and designers. Created strategic marketing plans and cultivated promotion and advertising partners.

ELECTRICFOOD.COM: Director of Content, Marketing, and Communications
January 2000–January 2001
Developed and produced retail food and entertainment website fully funded by one of nation's largest supermarket chains. Managed strategic partnerships with media companies and cross-promotions with product suppliers. Managed marketing, communications, and content production staff. Was responsible for placement in major consumer and trade media outlets. Produced and distributed newsletter, which increased sales by 300 percent.

Page 2

Lisa A. Johnson

L.A. COMMUNICATIONS: Media and Marketing Consultant
May 1995–January 2000
Produced content, promotions, and partnerships for clients such as
Fox News, Sundance, the *Salt Lake Tribune*, the *Deseret News*, *Salt
Lake City Magazine*, Clear Channel Broadcasting, and City Search.
Created marketing plans and public relations strategies for resorts,
restaurants, fashion designers, financial services companies, law
firms, public events, and Internet enterprises.

NEW ERA MAGAZINE: Editor
October 1985–May 1995
Conceived, wrote, and edited articles for international monthly
teenage magazine. Oversaw freelancers. Completely revamped
sections to make more reader-friendly and handled controversial
issues in print. Traveled extensively to cover stories all over the
world, especially in Spanish-speaking countries.

**EDUCATION
AND
TRAINING**
Bachelor of Arts in Communications, 1980, journalism emphasis,
Cum Laude, Brigham Young University, 1980

Additional Training:
Folio Seminars, Chicago, 1986; New York, 1989, 1993
Nikon School, 1993
Internet Marketing and Training Seminar, 1998

After:

LISA JOHNSON MANDELL

310-555-5555
ljmandell@gmail.com
www.lisajohnsonmandell.com

CAREER SUMMARY AND SKILLS

✓ Award-winning journalist with 15 years of professional experience in print, broadcast and Internet journalism, marketing, and public relations
✓ Published author and on-camera personality
✓ Broadcast film reporter and critic, with hundreds of major star interviews
✓ Food expert, restaurant reporter, and critic
✓ Fluent in Spanish
✓ Creator of video blog site LisaLiveinHollywood.com

PROFESSIONAL EXPERIENCE

IN HOLLYWOOD PRODUCTIONS: President
January 2001–present

TV, radio, Internet, and print content, production, public relations, and marketing materials, including numerous television news pieces as well as books, magazine articles, scripts, newsletters, and radio programming.
Clients:
Comcast, Fox News, Bravo, Greenstone Media, Tribute Entertainment, CitySearch .com, Forbes.com, the *Wall Street Journal*, the *New York Times*, the *Times* of London, AP, Random House, St. Martin's Press, CNBC, Paramount Domestic Television, KTLA, Dr. Phil, Rachael Ray, *Forbes*, Telemundo, Midwest Family Radio, Filmstew .com, the Learning Annex, and many others.

SUNDAY LUXURY: Editor in Chief
2005–2006

Created, marketed, launched, and promoted weekly magazine and corresponding website for affluent Los Angeles readers. Acquired and edited all content. Managed staff of writers, editors, columnists, photographers, and designers. Created strategic marketing plans and cultivated promotion and advertising partners.

AUTHOR: *HOW TO SNARE A MILLIONAIRE* (St. Martin's Press)

Became known as a relationship expert with numerous appearances on TV and radio talk shows, network news, and entertainment broadcasts. Currently appearing as a date coach on Bravo's hit reality series *Millionaire Matchmaker*.

ELECTRICFOOD.COM: Director of Content, Marketing, and
Communications
2000–2001

Developed and produced retail food and entertainment website for one of
nation's largest supermarket chains. Managed strategic partnerships with media
companies and cross promotions with product suppliers. Managed marketing,
communications and content production staff. Responsible for placement in major
consumer and trade media outlets.

LA COMMUNICATIONS: Media and Marketing Consultant
1995–2000

Produced content, promotions, and partnerships for Fox News, Sundance, *Salt
Lake Tribune*, *Deseret News*, Clear Channel Broadcasting, and City Search.
Created marketing plans and public relations strategies for resorts, restaurants,
fashion designers, financial services companies, law firms, public events, and
Internet enterprises.

EDUCATION

Bachelor of Arts in Communications, journalism emphasis, Cum Laude, Brigham
Young University, with additional seminars in magazine writing and publishing,
public relations, photography, Internet marketing and production.

INTERESTS AND ACTIVITIES

Member, Broadcast Film Critics Association; *world traveler* and international
journalist—covered stories on six of seven continents; *teen counselor*—worked
extensively with troubled youth; *humanities enthusiast*—avid historical fiction
reader, Western religion and art buff; *gourmet cooking*—attended classes in five
countries; *golfer* since age six, with varying handicap depending on the stakes;
public speaking—Learning Annex seminar leader, awards ceremonies keynote
speaker; *voiceover artist*—current character spot running for Time Warner;
and *dog park devotee*—in the company of our golden doodle pup "KC."

My résumé makeover included:

- Adding a photo to immediately get attention and emphasize that I'm fresh and hip (see guidelines for adding photos to résumés, page 170).
- Using alternate fonts and sizes for ease of reading.
- Deleting reference to my actual street address, and subbing in my Web address.
- Replacing the big block of "Career Summary" type with a bulleted list of "Career Summary and Skills."
- Removing graduation dates.
- Using a format that goes all the way across the page, instead of wasting space on the left with nothing more than headings.
- Popping up the "Interests and Activities" section with humorous additions—in the entertainment industry, it behooves you to let everyone know up front that you don't take yourself too seriously.

Here's one for an executive assistant or office manager. Diane started her career as a receptionist back in 1988, but ended up omitting her first several jobs.

Before:

Résumé

Diane Renee Sherwood
0000 Hayworth Ave. San Jose, CA 95128
(991) 000-0000
DianeRSherwood@gmail.com
DianeCanHelp.com

CAREER HIGHLIGHTS

More than 10 years of experience providing administrative and personal support to senior executives, partners, and CEOs.
Provided support and training to secretarial staff and new assistants by conducting office orientation and instructing new employees on filing procedures, computer applications, communications technologies, and public interface.
Resolved various employee and client issues, receiving commendations from managers, directors, and clients alike.
Was selected as "Employee of the Month" seven times and "Employee of the Year" twice.
Planned and organized travel, meetings, and special events.
Experienced in multitasking in a fast-paced environment, while maintaining an emphasis on professional relationships.
Managed multiline phone system, and employer's professional e-mail correspondence.

PROFESSIONAL EXPERIENCE

EXECUTIVE ASSISTANT to CEO, Canning Enterprises, Phoenix, AZ, 2004–2010: Provided support to CEO of company, which involved coordinating schedules, appointments, and travel arrangements; managed communication with employees, clients, board members, and public, including editing correspondence, speeches, reports, and press releases; assisted with company real estate transactions and setup and organization of satellite offices.

OFFICE MANAGER, Cormier Manufacturing, Chicago, IL, 1999–2004:
Managed and coordinated office staff consisting of five support workers, three managers, and two outside consultants; prioritized and delegated tasks, helping to increase office productivity by 40%; controlled budget, tracking office expenses and creating monthly reports; prepared invoices, accounts receivable/payable, and banking statements; resolved issues between employees and clients to the satisfaction of all involved.

ADMINISTRATIVE ASSISTANT, Selwyn and Parker, AZ, 1998–1999:
Mastered customer service duties, data entry, general office and receptionist responsibilities, managed office supplies and equipment, responded to client needs, and provided additional support where necessary.

EDUCATION

AAS, GENERAL BUSINESS, Glendale Community College, Glendale, AZ

ADDITIONAL SKILLS

Proficient in MS Office (Word, Excel, PowerPoint, Access), Windows NT/98/95, meeting planning, word processing, spreadsheets, database management, multiline phones, scheduling, office support, customer support, accounts payable, accounts receivable, invoices, benefits administration, office management, vendor/contractor relations.

- References available upon request

After:

Diane Renee Sherwood

DianeRSherwood@gmail.com
(991) 555-5555
ExtremeExecutiveAssistant.com

EXECUTIVE ASSISTANT/OFFICE MANAGER

Super Support Skills   Seasoned Arbitrator/Problem Solver   Detail-Oriented Pro

---

HISTORY

➤ Ten years of experience providing exceptional administrative and personal support to high-profile senior executives, partners, and CEOs.

➤ Provided support and training to secretarial staff and new assistants by conducting office orientation and instructing new employees on organization procedures, computer applications, communication technologies, and public interface.

➤ Resolved various employee and client issues, receiving commendations from managers, directors, and clients alike, including repeat recognition as "Employee of the Month" and "Employee of the Year."

===

PROFESSIONAL EXPERIENCE

EXECUTIVE ASSISTANT TO CEO

Canning Enterprises, Phoenix, AZ   2004–2010

Provided outstanding support to CEO of company, which involved coordinating schedules, appointments, and travel arrangements; managed communication with employees, clients, board members, and public, including editing correspondence, speeches, reports, and press releases; assisted with company real estate transactions, **set up and organized satellite offices**.

OFFICE MANAGER

Cormier Manufacturing, Chicago, IL   1999–2004

Managed and coordinated office staff consisting of five support workers, three managers, and two outside consultants; prioritized and delegated tasks, **helped increase office productivity by 40%**; controlled budget, tracked office expenses, and created monthly reports; prepared invoices, accounts receivable/payable, and banking statements; resolved issues between employees and clients to the satisfaction of all involved.

Diane R. Sherwood, p2.

ADMINISTRATIVE ASSISTANT

Selwyn and Parker, Springfield IL.   1998–1999
Exemplary customer service, data-entry, general office, and receptionist responsibilities, **managed office equipment**, responded to client needs, and provided additional support where necessary.

EDUCATION

AAS, General Business   Glendale Community College, Glendale AZ

ADDITIONAL SKILLS

Software
Proficient in MS Office (Word, Excel, PowerPoint, Access), meeting planning, word processing, spreadsheets, database management.
Office
Phone software, scheduling, office support, customer support, accounts payable, accounts receivable, invoices, benefits administration, office management, vendor/contractor relations.

AFFILIATIONS / PERSONAL INTERESTS

- Member, Big Brothers/Big Sisters
- 5–10K marathoner in connection with volunteer work for Habitat for Humanity
- Member, Mystery Book Club
- Gourmet Italian food chef (on occasion)

Diane's résumé makeover included:

- Determining her standout skills and featuring them right at the top.
- Deleting home address and subbing in Web address (after getting a more "searchable" Web address).
- Shortening her "Career Highlights" to make them more likely to be read than simply scanned.
- Adding a few buzzwords to telegraph confidence and sparkle, like "exceptional," "high-profile," "excelled," and "outstanding."
- Using one font for headings and another for body copy, making for a more pleasing and organized page scan.
- Adding a couple of very simple graphic elements from the Borders and Shading menu of Word to make the page more attractive and add white space.
- Highlighting a few standout phrases in the body of her work history detail.
- Eliminating run-on phrases that are tired or dated, like "NT98/95," "multiline phones," and "mastered customer service duties."
- Adding a couple of items regarding her personal interests, skills, and hobbies outside of the office.

Jennifer was looking for a managerial position in the health and/or beauty industry.

Before:

Jennifer McKay

(212) 000-0000
000 Kensington Ave., Apt. B
East Meadow, NY, 11554
JennyMckay@yahoo.com
TheBeautyLine.com

OBJECTIVE: To increase sales by focusing on account management, client relations, and the bottom line.

SUMMARY: Dynamic sales executive with accomplishments that include:

- 14+ years of experience of increasing responsibilities in sales positions.
- Built successful sales team from ground up, training associates in client relations skills, negotiating, and closing deals.
- Introduced products to new markets and established client services there.
- Cultivated long-lasting relationships with client base and identified new customer demographics.
- Conceived and implemented original sales promotions that boosted sales and awareness of specific products by 22%.
- Wrote effective sales pitch script for phone-in customers.

SPECIAL SKILLS

- Persuasive sales techniques: Communicates with creativity, enthusiasm, and sincerity to cultivate loyal, satisfied customers.
- Organization: Able to implement sales plans logically, from start to finish, and document every step of the way.
- Flexibility: Able to identify the need for change and resourcefully adapt. Always has a plan B, C, or D ready.
- Management: Able to find to find, hire, motivate, and supervise ideal sales associates and support staff.
- Customer Service: Able to accurately and promptly assess and fulfill customer needs.
- Budget Maximization: Effectively utilizes finite resources for infinite results.
- Computer Savvy: Fluent on both Mac and PC, expert in Word, Excel, PowerPoint, QuickBooks, and other programs, extreme Internet skills.

EMPLOYMENT HISTORY

Number One Cosmetics, 2004–2009, Senior Account Supervisor
Florentine Hair Care Products, 2002–2004, Account Manager
Proveen Health and Beauty, 1998–2002, Sales Associate
L'Express International, 1996–1998, Sales Associate

EDUCATION & TRAINING

BS, Health and Nutrition, University of Rochester, Rochester, NY
Number One Cosmetics Beauty Seminar, Chicago, IL
Primero International Health and Beauty Conference, Denver, CO
Beauty International Society, Management Circle

INTERESTS

Travel—Air Force brat, lived in Guam and Germany
Music—Sings in community choir
Philanthropy—Member of opera guild, volunteers with Make-A-Wish
Animals—Volunteers with the Humane Society, rescued a cat and two dogs

After:

Jennifer McKay

New York, NY
(212) 555-5555
JennyMcKay21@yahoo.com   www.JMBeautyLine.com

Expertise in Beauty and Cosmetics Sales and Management

Objective:
To help create a dynamic sales environment by focusing on account management, client relations, and a steady increase in the bottom line.

Core Strengths

Motivational Leader
Persuasive Sales Techniques
Keenly Aware of Current Market Trends
Attention to Vendor Relations
Uncommon Loyalty and Reliability

Education & Seminar Training

BS, Health and Nutrition, University of Rochester, Rochester, NY.
Computer Savvy: Fluent on both Mac and PC, expert in Word, Excel, PowerPoint, QuickBooks, and more.
Extreme Internet skills

Continuing Seminars & Memberships:
Number One Cosmetics Beauty Seminar, Chicago, IL
Primero Health & Beauty Conference, Denver, CO
Beauty International Society,
Management Circle

Personal Interests

Travel
Air Force brat, lived in Guam and Germany for 4 years each. Visted and/or backpacked 12 other countries
Music
Current member, West End Community Choir
Philanthropy
Member, City Center Opera Guild
Red Cross volunteer
Animals
Member, Humane Society, with two cat rescues, Mojo and Schmoopy

Experience

Dynamic sales executive with accomplishments that include:

▶14 + years of increasing responsibilities and results in national sales and sales management.
▶Built successful sales teams from ground up, training associates in client relations skills, negotiating, and closing deals.
▶Introduced products to new markets and established comprehensive client services.
▶Cultivated long-lasting relationships with client base and identified new customer demographics.
▶Wrote effective sales pitch scripts for phone-in customers.
▶Conceived and implemented original sales promotions that consistantly boosted sales by 20–40%.

Employment History

Senior Account Supervisor, First Blush Cosmetics, Princeton, NJ	2004–2009
Account Manager, Florentine Hair Care Products, Riverdale, NY	2002–2004
Sr. Sales Associate, Proveen Health & Beauty, NY, NY	1998–2002
Sales Associate, L'Express International, Brooklyn, NY	1996–1998

Special Skills

▶Persuasive sales techniques: Communicates with creativity, enthusiasm, and sincerity to cultivate loyal, satisfied customers.
▶Organization: Able to implement sales plans logically from start to finish and document every step of the way.
▶Flexibility: Skilled at identifying the need for change and resourcefully adapting. Always ready with Plan B, C, or D.
▶Management: Able to find, hire, motivate, and supervise ideal sales associates and support staff.
▶Budget Maximization: Effectively utilizes finite resources for infinite results.

Jennifer's résumé makeover included:

- Deciding on a standout format to match her standout personality.
- Simply listing her recent job history without comment on the functional side.
- Using a headline to set the tone.
- Mixing fonts and bullets for additional impact.
- Making the page interesting and dynamic by conveying her personality and drive.
- Creating this résumé in Quark Xpress, a page layout program that takes some skill to use. Remember, there are many affordable "résumé doctors" who can create similar or even more striking designs for very reasonable rates.
- When opting for a nonconventional layout such as this, remember that it will not scan well for electronic submissions and is meant for direct e-mailing as a PDF attachment or as a snail mail enclosure. You will want to have an additional simple text version of this résumé to paste into a potential employer's online application form or résumé file.

To Add a Photo or Not to Add a Photo?

You'll note that I added a photo to my résumé so that it is the first thing you see. That worked well for me, since I was applying for positions that would put me in the public eye, and the photo immediately shouted, "I am not old and frumpy—I am fresh and hip!" But that doesn't work for everyone. See the e-mail I received below for the answer I give about whether or not you should put your photo on your résumé:

Hello Lisa,

I've been working on getting my wife's résumé updated as she's been downsized a couple of times lately, and since you had success with the photo inclusion, I thought it might be a good idea for her, too. She is an executive assistant, working primarily for company presidents and senior-level executives.

We put a very tasteful and attractive photo of her in business attire (mostly head/shoulders shot) on the résumé, and are ready to send it out. But here's the *problem*: I'm now reading tons and tons of "Don't put photos on résumés!" articles on the Web. The reasons range from "it would look tacky" to "HR people are told to discard these for EOE [equal opportunity employer] reasons. They don't want to get sued."

Now, obviously your experience worked for you. But did you hear any of the same warnings from people before going this route? I know these types of warnings are probably just repeated by rote by many who aren't really in a position to know, but I'm just wondering about your experiences. I guess you can see that I'm looking for some reassurance! I have to say, though, that any more bites on her résumé would be welcomed at this point, since the market isn't great right now.

So, any thoughts would be greatly appreciated.

Rick

Dear Rick—

It's a good question you pose, and there are indeed a number of schools of thought on the subject. The picture worked well for me because I'm in the media/creative field, and would often need to represent the company to the public in some way. I believe a picture would be superfluous on the résumé if your wife is in a less visually oriented field, such as finance, medicine, tech, etc. In your wife's case, as a high-level executive assistant, I would suggest *not* adding the photo, but using that great photo you took of her on a blog, and putting the link to the blog near the top of her résumé. That should definitely get her past the first screening. You're right, there still are some companies out there that will reject résumés with photos for the reasons you mentioned. To make the résumé look fresh, however, you might consider deleting her date of graduation and any work experience more than fifteen years old.

You can set up a blog with that photo in about half an hour, on a site such as Blogger.com, Blogher.com, etc. Your wife can put entries on it such as "Top Ten Qualities Executives Look For in Assistants," "Secret Mistakes You Don't Want to Make in the Workplace," etc. Entries like that can be taken from your wife's personal experience, or she can mention an article she's seen recently and include a link to give the author credit. That way, if appearance is relevant to the position, the HR rep can go to the blog and not only see the flattering picture, but discover that your wife is current and at the top of her game.

Best of luck to you and your wife, and congrats on being such a supportive husband!

Lisa

As I've noted, including a photo is a dicey subject. Many larger employers use specific guidelines in order to maintain fair employment standards and to avoid any prejudicial bias. In fact, some immediately reject photo résumés to avoid the merest hint of impropriety. That said, I believe you need every edge you can get in this intensely competitive job market.

A RÉSUMÉ STRATEGY FOR APPLYING TO A SMALL COMPANY

If you're applying for a small-business position, the rules are up for more casual interpretation. You may be writing directly to the owner of the company instead of an HR division serving a 10,000-person corporation. Government and large corporations aside, here's a two-step approach worth considering when applying for a job at a smaller or less structured company:

Apply with your reworked résumé and cover letter first. If two or three weeks go by without a response, send an e-mail with your small photograph placed above the signature. It may make all the difference in catching someone's attention and getting you the interview that hasn't otherwise come. A photograph is a dynamic and unique presentation of who you are and the energy and beauty you exude. You're not going to get arrested for sending one. And in the right circumstance, it may be the specific tipping point you need to get an employer to pick up the phone. As my husband said to me when he first insisted I try this very powerful tactic: "Honey, this is war!"

Target Your Résumés

It's also a good idea to create a different résumé for each position or field. For example, a marketing expert might have one résumé for PR-oriented jobs, another for marketing positions, and a third for work that is more directed toward advertising. Someone looking for a managerial position might have one résumé for commercial companies, and one for nonprofit organizations. As a journalist, I have one résumé that's geared toward print, one toward the Internet, and one toward television/radio. With digital copies of your résumé saved and safely filed away on your computer, this doesn't take half the time it used to.

THE BIGGEST, MOST COMMON, AND MOST EASILY CORRECTED MISTAKE

The number one mistake people make when submitting their résumés by e-mail or online? Titling their Word résumé document simply "Resume.doc." How is an employer, dealing with a long list of attachments from many applicants, supposed to organize and process résumés quickly and efficiently when they all have the same title? Always, *always* use your own name when you title your résumé, something like "Lisa Johnson Mandell.doc." Many employers just delete all submissions simply slugged "Résumé" and move on, figuring if job candidates are not savvy enough to properly label their most precious submissions, how are they going to handle work files at that particular company?

Creative Cover Letters

The cover letter is a brief smile, a look in the eye, a firm handshake on paper. The shorter and sweeter the better. Most employers seldom get beyond the first paragraph in a cover letter, so you really have only a few minutes to make a positive first impression.

Whatever you do, don't blow all that Botox you used on your résumé by beginning with something like, "I have twenty years of experience in the field of…" A summary of your résumé looking back on all your experience is never a good idea either. You want to look forward in your cover letter, teasing your potential employer with the professional glory that is you.

You can't do that in a generic, one-size-fits all paragraph like, "Thanks for the opportunity to apply for the position at your firm. For your convenience, I've attached my résumé. I appreciate your time and consideration and look forward to hearing from you." Even if you customize it with the company name and the title of the position, it still sounds dull, unoriginal, and uninspiring. It won't help you stand out from the hundreds of other applications being received.

So let's begin at the beginning. Rather than starting with "Dear," "To Whom It May Concern," or, heaven forbid, "Hi," it's best to begin your letter with "Greetings"—it avoids awkwardness and is always appropriate, especially when you don't know the name of the person who is going to process your letter and résumé. Plus, if a person named something like Lynn Swanson is to receive your résumé, you don't know if it's a male or a female, so "Mr. or Ms. Swanson" is out, and "Lynn" is too informal for a first contact.

After the greeting, your great cover letter should contain the following elements:

■ Start the body of the cover letter with a reference to the specific job you're applying for, and include a reference code if there is one. Something like, "I'm very interested in the position of Director of Public Relations at American Bandersnatch, reference #53239." I advise putting the job title and reference code in the subject of the e-mail. Make sure you include the name of the specific company.

■ Then mention the person, website, or job board that referred you: "Jabberwocky CEO Lewis Carroll suggested I send my résumé your way." Or if no one referred you, begin with a positive comment about the company, such as, "I saw the listing on Monster.com, I've always admired your frumious bandersnatches, and would be thrilled to add my skills and experience to the company that has such a flawless history of manufacturing and marketing them."

■ Now write a sentence or two that emphasizes what you can do for them. They don't care about what they can do for you. So instead of saying something like, "I'm extremely interested in a position where I can grow and learn, utilizing my exceptional talents and abilities," say something like, "I believe my proven talents and unique experience in the promotion and marketing of bandersnatches could be invaluable assets to your team."

■ Add another sentence telling them how good you are at executing the duties mentioned in the ad: "I've had great success marketing and promoting bandersnatches in the past, increasing sales by more than 50 percent." Be sure to use the *same specific* verbiage used in the ad.

■ Now state the obvious: "For your convenience, I have attached [or included, if you're faxing or using snail mail] my résumé. Please let me know if you have any difficulties opening the document [if you're e-mailing—sometimes Mac and PC docs don't translate well]."

Now it's time for the big finish. In the last paragraph thank the employer for his/her time and consideration, and write that you're looking forward to hearing from them (or meeting with them) soon. This is not being pushy, it's just being positive, optimistic, and stating a fact. A good sign-off is "Best" or "All the Best." "Sincerely" or "Yours Truly" will make you look like your grandmother. It's time to abandon many of the lessons she taught you about writing thank-you notes.

Remember, short and sweet—no more than three quick paragraphs, and fewer than 300 words. If it's an attractive job you're applying for, the employer will be overwhelmed with applications, and you don't want yours to appear burdensome, pretentious, or, worst of all, old.

Finally, your résumé will often be the first impression you make on an employer, so it is one of the most important aspects of your job search. Résumés and cover letters are smoking-hot topics, and I've just covered a few basics here. While I think I've been effective in sending you on your way, you'll find dozens and *dozens* of books devoted to the subject at your library and bookstore, and you'll find many more articles online. It wouldn't hurt to spend an hour or two browsing other sources, just in case I've left anything out that is pertinent to your particular field. You can never be overeducated on this topic, and you're bound to come away with some excellent—and valuable—ideas.

Now that you've created a killer résumé that makes prospective employers stand up and say, "Howdy!" it's time to meet them face-to-face. The next chapter will teach you how to handle your interview like the smooth professional you are, and leave them dying to sign you on the dotted line.

9

Interview Like a Rock Star

In business, you don't get what you deserve, you get what you negotiate.

—*Chester L. Karrass*

Your killer résumé and all that social networking have finally paid off in a big way: You've scheduled an interview for your dream job at the ideal company in the perfect location. Only problem is, the night before was a night*mare*. You were so excited you couldn't sleep until you finally nodded off at 5:00 a.m. and slept right through your 7:00 a.m. alarm. You're standing knee-deep in a pile of clothes and not having any luck putting together that fabulous interview ensemble. Meanwhile, you have less than thirty minutes to eat breakfast, shower, do your makeup, print out a copy of your résumé, and MapQuest directions to the interview location. Just try and arrive cool, confident, and capable under those circumstances!

Relax! I'm about to show you how to avoid all that, and to ace the interview with ease and grace. After you're done with this chapter, you'll not only stop dreading interviews, but you'll actually look forward to them as your favorite part of the entire job-hunting process. To be honest, the interview is definitely *my* favorite part. If I can just get my foot in the door, I feel like I'm home free and can relax and start having fun. What's not to like about it? I enjoy dressing up, I enjoy meeting new people, I enjoy the challenge of trying to ascertain what the potential employer wants and then giving it to him or her, if I decide it's in my best interest. And my comfort and confidence with the interview process gets amazing results. I've had companies call me back and leave a job offer in my voice mail before I've even had time to drive home from the interview.

Just because an interview is fun, however, doesn't mean it's easy. It's not uncommon for me to spend a full week preparing for an interview, as I did recently. For that particular position, I did extensive research on the publishing company and compiled and made color copies of a number of magazine and Web articles I'd written. I also brainstormed a variety of fresh ideas for their new news source, in case they asked for some. I boned up on the latest in every subject I thought we might discuss, and researched East Coast corporate culture, since the company's headquarters was in Washington, D.C., and as you may or may not know, East Coast corporate dress standards and West Coast dress standards are not just a continent apart but worlds, even universes, apart.

In D.C., New York, and Boston a conservative, dark-colored suit for an interview would be acceptable. In L.A., even the valets would laugh at you if you were dressed like that. I put a lot of thought and effort into an outfit that would be appropriate for a Southern California gal to wear to an interview conducted by an East Coast professional on the West Coast. The solution: conservative chic, with a bit of Hollywood glamour thrown in. I was being considered for a position as a Hollywood specialist. I knew it would be best to look the part. I wore a chocolate brown, full-skirted, knee-length surplice dress, accented it with a wide suede leopard belt, gold necklace, a bronze metallic Michael Kors tote, and pretty beige peep-toe pumps (remembering what my model mother told me about shoes roughly the same color as your skin making your legs look longer and slimmer). I knew I would need the kind of outfit that would look equally appropriate having high tea at the Beverly Wilshire, going to a studio cocktail party, doing an on-camera celebrity interview, or...interviewing for a job as a Hollywood insider.

I arrived at the interview a good fifteen minutes early and had plenty of time to compose myself, check my hair and makeup in the ladies' room, etc. When it came time to meet the CEO and his assistant, I looked them both in the eye and deferred to them both—I knew the assistant would be putting her two cents' worth in after I left. Whatever I wore, said, or did seemed to impress them.

A few days later I received a phone call in which they told me that what they really had in mind was starting a gossip blog, but because they didn't think I'd deign to write about the inanities of celebrity underwear and such, they'd decided to start an entirely different film-focused website, and wanted me to launch and run it using my invaluable skills and connections. They hadn't given a thought to my age—I appeared young and hip enough to them, and my blog site, LisaLiveInHollywood.com, which I'd launched only a few months before, had exactly the kind of voice they were seeking. That was all that mattered to them. Several months later they told me they were absolutely stunned when they saw me on NBC's *Today* show and heard Matt Lauer announce to the world that I was forty-nine. They had assumed a younger person was running the site. I was actually older than any of the people who hired me! And no, they didn't fire me as soon as they discovered my true age. They were perfectly happy with the work I was doing at that point.

I'm not telling you this to brag, I'm telling you this to prove a point: In an interview, or in an entire career, actual age is irrelevant. It's the vibrancy, confidence, and enthusiasm that are often associated with youth that make the biggest difference. Arm yourself with these qualities and you'll ace your interviews every time. And what's more, you'll actually enjoy them!

Look Like a Million

Without trying to sound superficial or clichéd here, it's true that you don't get a second chance to make a first impression. And the first impression you make almost always is a result of the way you look. Plus, it's a delicious little circle: When you look confident, you feel confident. When you feel confident, you look confident. So why not start with the way you look? When you walk into that interview, you want to give the impression that "She's a force to be dealt with! If we don't snatch her up immediately, someone else will!" Don't laugh—you *are* a force to be dealt with, and you're perfectly capable of conveying that message!

So often we go into interviews, proverbial hat in hand, almost feeling like beggars, radiating the message, "Please give me this job, please, please, *please* give me this job. I'll do anything!" But those self-deprecating days are over for you. You're going to take one last look at yourself when you walk out the door, and you are going to say to yourself, "Wow! I am stunning! They are going to consider themselves infinitely lucky to snare me, and they're going to raise the pay level just to keep me interested!" The first step to feeling like you're worth a million is to look like a million, and you don't have to spend a million to achieve that look.

If you've already gone through your closet as I advised in chapter 4, you should have gotten rid of all those stodgy blue suits and cream shells, and invested in more up-to-date and vibrant career wear. I know, I know, there are still websites out there that encourage you to go for that stuffy, ultraconservative business suit, but in a word, they are *wrong*! Look at the prominent women who were, in a way, interviewing for some of the highest offices in the world in the last election— Hillary Clinton, Sarah Palin, and Michelle Obama. (It sounds funny to put those three in the same sentence now, doesn't it?) My point being that you never caught them in plain navy suits with dull white blouses. If their outfits were good enough for the prospective president, First Lady, and vice president of the United States, I would think they'd be good enough for most mere mortal job interviews. Now, I'm not saying that you should wear red, orange, or canary yellow pantsuits to your interviews, or that you should spend hundreds of thousands of dollars on a brand-new, designer career wardrobe. I'm just saying that pops of color and style help you stand out and make you memorable. You don't want your appearance to be distracting, but you do want it to leave an unforgettable impression, even when you're interviewing for more conservative positions in fields such as banking and law.

You also don't want your appearance to be the object of derision, which is exactly how you come across when you go in for an interview in a casual work environment, wearing a formal business suit. It's true that it's better to overdress than to underdress for an interview, but in some instances that classic business suit just makes you look like you're trying too hard and that you haven't done your homework on the corporate environment. The veteran employees as well as the up-and-comers will laugh at you.

My advice to you is to visit the venue where you'll be interviewing, if at all possible, and see what other employees who would be in a similar position are wearing. It's best not to do it on a Friday, of course, when employees might be dressed down, but a little reconnaissance ahead of time will also help you in other respects, like letting you know where to park or which subway to take, and how long it will take you to get there from your home or office. The more knowledge you have beforehand, the more comfortable, calm, and relaxed you will be when the actual interview time approaches. If you're interviewing in another city and find it impossible to visit the workplace ahead of time, make a call to the human resources department, where you'll no doubt find someone who would be happy to make suggestions about the proper interview attire. Chances are that person will not only give you invaluable information, but will be impressed with your resourcefulness and report it to the person who will be doing the interview.

PROFESSIONAL ADVICE

SHOULD YOU SKIRT THE ISSUE?

There's a great deal of debate these days over whether a skirt or pants would be the best interview choice. While many female recruiters, human resources reps, and executives wear pants to interviews, I still say go for the skirt whenever possible. I know it sounds sexist and appears to make gender an issue, but while there's the slim chance that some archaic organizations consider pants on a woman to be inappropriate, you'll always be appropriate wearing a skirt. In addition, it shows a degree of confidence and distinction to dress like a woman (provided you are one, of course). Anyone can take the easy route and wear pants, but you will distinguish yourself in a positive way by "dressing up" for the occasion in a skirt. If you're really not comfortable in a skirt, the most important thing is to look "put together" or "well coordinated," whether you're wearing a suit or any other professional-looking outfit.

Interview Dressing Do's and Don'ts

Do wear:

- Conservative jewelry that doesn't get in the way or catch on anything.

- A simple manicure—neutral-colored or clear, rounded nails that are not too long.

- A clean, simple hairstyle. Long hair hanging down is fine if it's shiny and healthy, but don't allow it to get in your eyes. I hate to say this, but if you want to appear vibrant and fresh, you'll cover the gray. You'll be surprised to find that some of your thirty-year-old coworkers are doing the same thing.

- Light, fresh-looking makeup, with tinted lip gloss, only—no dark-colored lips allowed. Think of the joy and freedom of not having to worry about lipstick on your teeth.

- Tailored skirt, dress, or pants of a quality fabric that fits well and won't easily wrinkle.

- Polished, unscuffed, comfortable shoes. Heels are fine, if they're comfy and in good shape. Brand-new, previously unworn shoes could give you blisters as you walk from the parking lot to the building or travel on public transportation, and you'll look really cute hobbling down the hall to your interview. Break in your new interview shoes before the big day.

■ Stylish messenger bag, portfolio, or tote, preferably made of leather (see chapter 4).

■ If you must wear socks with your shoes when you're wearing pants, make sure the socks are of the thin, trouser variety and knee-high. Socks should never be lighter than your dress pants, and should never allow skin to show when you cross your legs.

■ Knee-length skirts or ones that hit just above or below the knee are best. Too long looks frumpy, too short is not appropriate, no matter how great your legs look.

■ Something to cover tattoos. You might be able to get away with them in a hair salon, but they tend to draw attention in an interview situation when all the focus should be on you and your abilities. The same goes for rings or studs in piercings anywhere other than your ears.

■ Bare legs. But if you absolutely *must* wear stockings, make sure they're either so sheer they look invisible, or opaque and colored enough to be considered tights.

Don't wear:

■ Large, dangly, or otherwise prominent earrings, or flashy bling. This includes oversized rings. You may be able to get away with them later when you've already nailed the job, but initially don't distract the interviewer with your jewelry.

■ Bright- or dark-colored long fingernails that look as if they might prohibit you from doing job duties.

■ Messy, wild hair, an elaborate updo, or an outdated haircut. If there's time, get a cut and style at a hip salon at least a week before the interview, or a professional blow-out the day of. Don't get your hair cut and colored the day before—we all know how we hate our hair the first day after.

■ Heavy, colorful makeup. Heavy makeup will call attention to the fact that you're trying to cover something up (like your age?).

■ Jeans or unstructured knit pants that could be mistaken for sweats or yoga pants. Also avoid linen and light cotton that wrinkle easily.

■ Tennis shoes, flip-flops, or scruffy-looking shoes that appear unkempt. Make sure your heels are in good condition, and not scuffed from driving your car. Also, pay attention to how they sound when you walk. This might sound odd, but you don't want to call attention to yourself striding through an office with heels, mules, or thongs that go slap, slap, slap when you walk.

■ Perfume. Heavy perfume is very 1980s, and the interviewer could be allergic to certain scents. Forget what you might have heard about leaving your signature scent behind—that only works on dates.

■ Chewing gum—no matter how bad your breath may be. Carry breath mints if you're in doubt.

■ Briefcase, backpack, or big, bright, floppy purse. No matter how high-quality it may be, the briefcase is far too masculine, the backpack is too casual, and the hobo bag is too frivolous.

■ Short or bulky socks with pants—no skin, wrinkles, rolls, or little pom-poms should show when you cross your legs.

■ Sunglasses on your head.

■ Miniskirts—that includes anything that hits six inches above the knee when standing. It's going to hike up to the upper thigh when sitting, and you don't want anyone hiring you for the wrong reasons.

■ Fishnets, patterned stockings, colored stockings, or heavy, flesh-colored panty hose.

■ Hats of any shape, size, or color.

■ Anything too froufrou or girly girl. This includes an overabundance of ruffles, lace, or bows. Pretty pastels from head to toe also fall into this category, as does anything too see-through, flimsy, or delicate. Anything that allows your bra to peek through is way off base.

The Night Before the Day Of

It's best to lay out exactly what you'll be wearing several days in advance, so you'll know if you need to get anything dry cleaned or if there's one more small accessory to acquire to complete your perfect look. It's totally unnerving when you notice perspiration odor on a blouse as you're putting it on and ready to walk out the door, or to realize that your dog chewed up the shoes that match the outfit you'd planned on wearing. If you've purchased new items, make sure all tags and extra buttons are removed. Be careful to check the soles of your shoes, where stores often paste sale stickers. The last thing you want to worry about is your appearance. Ideally you should focus your full concentration on your presentation and performance.

It's also important to prepack that stylish bag you've acquired with the following must-haves for any job interview:

■ At least $50 in cash so you can pay for parking, if necessary, or cab, subway, or bus fare. If you live in a smaller city you can carry less, but why not have enough to treat yourself afterward to a nice latte, to let off steam, so to speak?

■ Your driver's license and a passport if you have one, even if you didn't drive, because some job applications require a driver's license number and/or other proof of citizenship. Also, many buildings require you to show some form of ID to gain entrance.

■ An electronic device, address book, or list that contains the names, numbers, and addresses of your former employers and references, so you can fill out the job application easily, quickly, and completely.

■ If you're carrying a cell phone in your bag, make sure you turn it off before you enter the building. It's bad form to make a production of turning it off after you've been seated for the interview, and even worse to hear your ringtone in the middle of the interview, blaring "If I Were a Rich Girl."

■ A brush or comb so you can fix your hair in the ladies' room before your appointment.

■ Lip gloss to freshen your look.

■ Breath mints (not gum!) just in case.

■ A good pen that doesn't blob ink, to fill out your application.

■ Several extra copies of your résumé, printed on high-quality paper. Yes, you've probably already e-mailed your résumé in and a good interviewer will have it on hand, but just in case he or she doesn't, or you speak to more than one person, it looks extremely efficient for you to be able to pull out a fresh copy.

■ A list of references, also printed on high-quality paper, so you can leave it with the interviewer if requested.

■ Samples of your work, if applicable, such as articles you've written or have been featured in, a screenshot of your web or blog site, designs, spreadsheets, plans, drawings, etc. If possible, have color copies that you can leave behind for the interviewer to examine and show to others. If you're in radio or television, an extra audio and/or video demo is essential, even if you've already sent one.

PROFESSIONAL ADVICE

Muy Importante—Organization. Make sure everything is well organized in your bag and within easy reach. My friend Shauna accidentally pulled out a yellow-wrapped maxipad, then her plastic pill bottle full of antidepressants, on her way to producing the extra copy of her résumé the interviewer requested. Needless to say, she didn't get past the first interview.

GLOW WITHOUT THE GLITZ

Marie Monet, a celebrity makeup artist with her own cosmetics line who has worked on everyone from Joan Rivers to David Beckham, Carmen Electra to Raven-Symoné, knows just how to select the right look for any particular situation. She gives the following tips for the subdued look you'll want to adapt for your job interview:

■ Use muted or defused tones on the eyes—earth tones that are sheer in color. Stay away from bold, vibrant colors like blue or green.

■ A tinted brow gel will give shape and depth to your brows as well as make the eyes pop and give a finished and polished look. A pencil stroke can be too extreme.

■ If using eyeliner, use brown tones depending on your complexion. Stay away from black, which can give a harsh appearance.

■ Use a sheer lip color on your lips and avoid opaque colors and strong pigments such as bright red or coral. A naturally colored lip liner that matches your own, real lip color works best. Never use a dark lip liner.

■ Blush should be applied subtly from the apple on your cheek toward your hairline, accentuating your cheekbones.

Questions and Answers

You've scored that interview and you know exactly how you're going to look and what you're going to bring with you, but what are you going to say? You can figure this out by preparing some of your answers in advance, and coming up with a few intelligent questions of your own. In addition, you'll want to prepare your attitude in advance, and by this I mean the way you'll talk, act, and respond to questions. To give you an idea of what I'm talking about, I thought it would be helpful to share with you a few of the celebrity interview tricks I've learned over the years.

How to Interview a Movie Star

While I've probably been on less than a hundred job interviews, I've conducted at least a thousand celebrity interviews, and I've noticed quite a few similarities. It's every bit as intimidating to sit down for a one-on-one with a superstar like Leonardo DiCaprio as it is to sit down for an interview with any HR rep. My first celebrity interview ever was with Arnold Schwarzenegger, before he became the Governator. Now *that* was intimidating, and I wish I'd known then what I know now. He was the picture of politeness and chivalry, by the way. The rules of the interview game are pretty much the same no matter whom you're playing with, and if I can use them to make an impression and get what I need from a superstar, you can use them to make an impression and get what you need from a potential employer.

   1. Do your homework. Get the full name of the person who will be conducting the interview, and Google the hell out of that person and his or her company. Memorize as many facts as possible. You won't want to try to be impressive by showing how much you already know, but you will want to have those facts readily available if a pertinent reference comes up, or you have the opportunity to ask an intelligent question about it.

2. Look your absolute best. If you're not sure about the appropriateness, comfort, or fit of something, don't wear it. You want to be concentrating on the interview, not whether or not your skirt rides up when you sit down. Once, when interviewing figure skater Scott Hamilton, I made the egregiously age-inappropriate error of wearing a shortish denim skirt with Uggs. Scott was not exactly relating to me during the interview, and I didn't understand why until I saw the tapes afterward. When I crossed my legs, my skirt rode up so high my underwear—and my cellulite—were on humiliating display. I still cringe when I think about that.

3. Concentrate on making the other person comfortable, even if they astronomically outrank you. If you're trying to put the other person at ease, you won't have time to think about yourself and how nervous you are. (By the way, this is a trick I use in social settings as well.)

4. Handle the handshake issue with grace. When you first meet, look the person in the eye, notice whether or not the hand is extended to shake, and if it is, take it firmly, and say something like, "I'm very happy to meet you, Mr. DiCaprio." Always use the name by which he or she has been introduced when you greet them. People love hearing their own names, and repeating it will cement it in your own mind. Handshakes can be tricky these days. Some people, like Howie Mandell and Ashley Judd, would rather not touch you. Ashley is cagey—she either has her dog sitting in her lap and is busy futzing with it when you walk in, or she makes a show of putting lotion on her hands and massaging them together so you don't attempt to shake her hand. I've run into situations where the person I'm about to have an interview with tells me, "I'm getting over a really bad cold so you probably don't want to touch me." If this is the case, don't make a big deal out of it. Just politely smile and tell them, "Thank you—I appreciate that." Whatever you do, do not cup your left hand over their right when you're shaking, in a two-hand shake. This is far too intimate and informal.

5. Sit down only when and where you are invited to sit. If you are already seated when the other person enters the room, stand up, regardless of gender.

6. Mind your posture! I know I sound like your grandmother, but it's important to sit up straight with your shoulders back and your chin up, rather than slouched over with your head bent. Leaning forward a bit conveys interest and enthusiasm. Make eye contact if it's comfortable for both of you, and if it isn't, talk to the nose. Talking to the mouth can be too distracting, especially if the person you're interviewing with is good-looking. One look at Matthew McConaughey's sexy smirk and I'm a babbling idiot.

7. Come prepared with interesting, insightful questions of your own. If you did your homework, you should have a long list. Put the most important ones at the top of your list, and the lesser ones toward the bottom, in case you don't have time to get to them all.

8. Never, never interrupt. Wait until the other person has completely finished before you begin speaking.

9. Do not babble. Speak in complete, concise sentences, and refrain from using space fillers such as "ya know?" and "like." Bad example: "So I'm, like, really good with people, ya know?"

10. Don't be afraid of silence or pauses. Let the person you're talking to finish their thought, and do not rush in to fill pauses with banal conversation. I hate to say it, but this is often a gender thing. We women feel as if we need to facilitate conversation and keep it going at all times. Rent the film *Happy-Go-Lucky*, starring Sally Hawkins, for a great example of what *not* to do.

11. Steer clear of giving out personal information unless you are specifically asked for it. You are not there to discuss your family, your pets, your health, your intimate feelings or beliefs. Personal anecdotes and/or opinions that don't pertain directly to the subject at hand are indiscreet and inappropriate. This, by the way, will set you apart in a good way from the younger and less experienced candidates, who believe the world is fascinated by every detail of their personal lives. No matter what anyone has told you, you are *not* a walking reality show.

12. Do not leave until you are dismissed, and make sure you show gratitude. When an interview is finished, the person conducting the interview will generally thank you and/or stand up, indicating that it's time for you to leave. Thank him or her for consideration and for the time spent, even if you hated every minute of it. I'd rather have a four-hour total body wax than an interview with Tommy Lee Jones, but I respect him for taking the time to talk to me, and I tell him so. If in your job interview you decide you'd really like the job, mention that you look forward to hearing from them soon. This is not a push but a suggestion, and conveys confidence that you will, indeed, hear from them again soon.

Attitude is everything, with movie stars or with potential employers. You want to maintain a positive, confident demeanor, even if the interviewer is saying outrageous things that really push your buttons, or is asking you questions that bring up your worst pet peeves. Sometimes they do this on purpose, saying things like, "How would you handle it if you caught another employee stealing?" or "What was your worst boss like?" Direct all focus on your strengths, with no baggage opening allowed. Some people expect older candidates to be more negative, to complain that the good old days are over, and to be more bitter or impatient. In all fairness, we do have a lot more baggage than younger workers, but we need to remember to check that baggage at the door.

Ten Common Interview Mistakes

I asked a group of employers who frequently interview potential employees about their interview pet peeves. This is what they came up with:

1. Criticizing and complaining about past employers. This is not an opportunity to air dirty laundry. We just want to know why you're not employed there anymore.

2. Asking the interviewer personal questions. It's none of your business whether we're married or single, have children, etc. You are not trying to become our friend. Job interviews are strictly business.

3. Giving too much personal information. Younger people do this more than seasoned workers, but we'd rather not hear about your health, clothes, what you did last night with your roommates or your children.

4. Appearing too needy. We have actually interviewed people who have said, "I'll do anything to get this job!" Remember that while you may *want* this job, you do not *need* this job, no matter how dire your financial straits.

5. Putting hands in pockets or playing with ears, hair, or face. This connotes distraction, insecurity, and/or lack of interest. Keep your hands folded in your lap, or on the desk or table in front of you.

6. Pretending to understand the question then wasting time with a completely unrelated answer. It's okay to ask for clarification.

7. Displaying too much familiarity or flirtatiousness. We're not thinking about dating you, we're thinking about hiring you. Do not confuse the two.

8. Disinclination to talk about weaknesses. Do not, when asked, "What's your greatest weakness," say, "I can't think of any." The clever interviewee will flip a perceived weakness into a strength by saying something like, "Sometimes my enthusiasm for my work can annoy my coworkers," or "Since I'm extremely punctual, sometimes I become impatient with people who aren't."

9. Admitting, "I'm really nervous." We want someone who is cool and confident in tense situations. We don't want someone who is going to be nervous with important clients. Moreover, it implies you want us to take care of you and put you at ease—which is not our job at this point. If you need that much coddling and comforting in an interview, we get the impression you'll be too needy and uncomfortable on the job.

10. Being defensive about your age or experience. Stating, "I may not be as tech savvy as a twentysomething, but my work ethic is phenomenal," only stresses the fact that you're not tech savvy. Saying, "I don't have much experience in this particular field, but I have a wealth of experience in another," only red-flags the fact that you are not qualified for the job at hand.

PROFESSIONAL ADVICE

AVOID "UP-TALKING"

You hear a lot of people from Generation X and Y ending all their sentences on an up note, as if there's a question mark at the end of every sentence. This is a youthful speech pattern you should avoid, although it's extremely easy to pick up because it's so prevalent. It sounds something like this: "I have a friend who works here? And she really enjoys it?" "I left my last job because it wasn't really challenging? I couldn't see any room to advance?" If you do have teenagers at home, you'll be especially susceptible to this. Be aware of it and don't let it sneak into your own speech.

Be an Ageless Applicant

Be aware that interviewers will be looking for age-related issues. It's not pretty or fair, but unfortunately, it's a fact of life. No need to feel singled out and persecuted—everyone has to endure age bias, no matter where they are in life. Younger workers will have to prove they're mature and experienced enough just as older workers have to prove they're flexible and energetic enough. I'm going to give you a number of common questions employers ask to discern if older workers are right for the position. If you know what they're actually looking for, you can avoid making age an issue in your answers.

"Your experience indicates that you might be overqualified for this position. Do you think you are?" Sometimes the word "overqualified" actually translates to "old and expensive," so you should never admit to being overqualified, even if you feel that you could perform these job duties in your sleep. Start with, "Well, I do have some invaluable experience..." and then tell the interviewer what interests you about the job at this point in your career, and explain which of your qualifications would be particular assets to the position.

"Tell me about yourself." This seems innocent enough, but you could be tricked into presenting yourself as a smug veteran in the twilight of her career. Do not stress all your years of experience, but rather talk about the strengths and skills you've developed that relate to that particular job. If you've taken time off to raise kids, support your husband, whatever, this is not the time to bring it up. The interviewer will get to that and ask about it specifically. In the meantime, keep this answer short, sweet, and professional. No "long walks on the beach" type answers—your likes and dislikes are irrelevant.

"You haven't worked full-time for a while. Are you ready for a full-time position?" You'll be asked this if you've been freelancing, have recently graduated, or have taken a break to raise children, recover from an illness, care for an ailing family member, etc. Your answer to that should be twofold. Explain that while you've been very successful working independently in an unstructured environment, you miss working with a team to achieve a common goal. Then stress all the wonderful skills you developed raising a family, volunteering, caregiving, or working on your own to make ends meet.

"**Where do you see yourself professionally in the next ten to twenty years?**" They're obviously trying to assess how long before you plan on retiring, and whether you're just biding your time until you do or are sincerely interested in moving ahead and improving. Use phrases like "positions of increased responsibility," "stay on the cutting edge of my field," "building on experience," and "increasing momentum."

"**I see some gaps here in your job history. Tell me about them.**" Be honest and talk about the work skills you developed during those gaps. For example, if you were running a household, you managed complex schedules and financial issues. You developed flexibility, resourcefulness, and the ability to keep your cool while handling emergencies of all types. You also developed communications skills with diverse groups of all ages.

"**How do you feel about being supervised by someone who is younger than you are?**" Elaborate on how you enjoy working with people of all ages, and that you find youthful energy to be contagious and motivating. Give examples from your recent work history, if they apply.

"**You were probably at a higher salary level at your last job than you would be here. How would you feel about that?**" If you already know the pay scale is something you can live with but it's lower than you'd expected and you still want the job, you might want to say something like, "I'm not unaware of the added value of corporate benefits," or "In today's economy, we all have to make a few concessions." By the way, you can still say those things even if the salary is surprisingly higher than you'd anticipated. It's all about your perceived worth. If you don't have any idea what the pay range is, now is the time to ask. If it's so low you couldn't possibly accept it, you could ask about bonuses and incentives, and if those are nonexistent or unacceptable to you, simply tell them, "I'm sorry, that's not quite what I anticipated. I appreciate your time and consideration, but I'm sure there are other candidates better suited to the position. Thank you." Then graciously make your exit.

"We use some pretty sophisticated technology here. Would you require much training or could you jump right in?" They're basically trying to find out how tech savvy you are, and I don't think you would have gotten as far as the first interview if you didn't already have many of the skills required. This is where all my harping on building your own web or blog site will serve you extremely well—you'll have "living" proof that you know your way around the Internet. Give point-by-point examples of the tech skills you do have, and finish it off with "I understand each company has its own unique systems and methods, but I'm extremely flexible, adaptable, and a very quick learner. I don't anticipate any problems at all hitting the ground running." That is, unless you have absolutely no idea what they're doing there, and would require extensive training. Then you focus on the flexible, quick-learner part.

"Most of our employees are in a different age group. Would that make you uncomfortable?" Stress that you are a team player, and that age makes no difference to you. You're also eager to learn, and believe that anyone, of any age, has important information to share. If you can think of any examples from your past experience that show how age diversity has been an asset, now is the time to pull them out.

"Do you have any questions?" Whatever you do, do not tell them, "No—I think you've pretty much covered everything." That would show you're neither curious nor particularly interested, both negative traits that are sometimes unjustly associated with older workers. This is a good time to demonstrate that you've done your homework on your potential employer, and even if you don't have any questions about the particular job, you can ask questions about the overall company. Asking about salary at this point is dicey, however. The interviewer should bring this up, and if the subject hasn't been broached already, it's because either someone else will bring it up in a second interview (woo-hoo!) or you haven't made the first cut (boo-hoo!). You'll know soon enough. It's important to maintain your dignity—you never know when they might think of you for another position.

Lisa's ADVICE

ABOVE ALL, BUILD BRIDGES

When I returned to Los Angeles from Utah after just having turned forty, I went to interview for a position with Warner Bros. in their film publicity department. It involved writing PR materials and it carried what I thought was a phenomenal salary at the time. While I loved each staff member I met and the work environment seemed idyllic, it became apparent to everyone involved, including myself, that I wasn't qualified. I was gracious, however, asked lots of questions, and left on a very positive note, even though I knew I didn't have a snowball's chance in hell of getting the job. About four years later I received an e-mail from one of the people I'd met during that interview, inviting me to apply for another position at Warner Bros. I was stunned that they remembered me. I couldn't help but recognize the power of the positive interview, and the ability to ask, and answer, all the right questions.

Follow Up

No matter whether you feel that you aced the interview and will inevitably receive a job offer, or that you totally blew it and pray you'll never run into any of those people on the street, you must absolutely, positively send a follow-up thank-you message just as soon as you get home. Make it a quick, prompt response that is efficient and not overeager or apologetic. Short and sweet is best, something like:

Greetings [Interview Person],
    I really enjoyed meeting with you today and learning more about your fascinating company. I was especially intrigued by [name one aspect of the interview]. I think this could be a great fit. I look forward to hearing from you soon.
                                    All the best,
                                    Your Name

Note that the same rules apply to the thank-you note as to the cover letter. "Greetings" solves the awkward problem of a greeting that begins with "Hi" (too informal) or "Dear" (too intimate). Also, "All the best" solves the dilemma of whether to write "Sincerely," or "Yours Truly," either of which would peg you as old and unoriginal. If you don't have an e-mail address for the interviewer, although I can't imagine that happening in this day and age, handwriting a note and sending it the old-fashioned way, by snail mail, will suffice, but make sure your handwriting is really good—few people are used to reading handwriting these days. You could always print out the thank-you note on your own letterhead, and sign it with a black ink pen. That looks extremely professional.

The Waiting Game

This is probably the most difficult part of the entire interview process, at least for me. I have very little patience, and prefer that everything be done yesterday. If you don't hear back from the company in the time you were told you would, feel free to check in, either by phone or e-mail, but don't call and pester them before then. Your thank-you note was sufficient to remind them of your interest in the job. Remember that government agencies and large corporations can take much longer to make a hire—sometimes you'll be left in the dark for up to two months, so don't start panicking at the two-week mark. But don't halt your job search, either. You should continue submitting résumés until the day you sign your employment contract or start work at your new job. You never know what might happen at the last minute—the company could suddenly go under, the person you're replacing could decide she wants her old job back, your new boss could have a heart attack—virtually anything could arise these days. Look at all the financial specialists who lost their jobs right after they were hired in the fall of 2008.

That All-Important Salary Issue

Best-case scenario, the company you interviewed with gets back to you promptly, invites you in for another interview, does a background check, and then makes a job offer. Know that you are not home free quite yet. Along with the job offer comes a salary offer, and trying to figure out what's going to work best in that regard can be excruciating!

I'd be willing to bet that anyone who has ever been to a job interview has had the misfortune to be asked by a lame interviewer, "So what kind of a salary are you looking for?" That is usually an inappropriate and unprofessional question, and it puts you in the most awkward of positions, but you can't stop anyone from asking it. You squirm, because you know that if you state a figure that's too high, they may write you off and hire someone else who comes cheaper, and if you state a figure that's too low, they may try and take advantage of you by hiring you for less than they'd intended to pay you. It's appropriate to answer that question with a question, something like, "I'm not sure yet what the position entails. What salary range are you offering?" If pressed, an all-encompassing answer could be, "It's negotiable, depending on the responsibilities of the position and the benefits that go with it." Don't let anyone intimidate you into stating the first number.

In many situations, you know the salary range when you apply—it was one of the factors that influenced your submission of an application in the first place. But it's always good to be prepared for the discussion by researching salary levels for similar positions in your area. This kind of information is easy to come by on the Internet—Glassdoor .com is especially useful. Sometimes you'll be asked about your salary history, either in person or on an application. When you answer this question, be honest, but make sure you add in the full value of your benefits, including what your employer paid for your health insurance, the company contribution to your 401(k), and any stock options. With the really high-level executive positions, the subject of salary will not even be broached in the first interview. They'll try to discern what they want to offer you. I've also been in situations where the executive interviewing me sends me down to an HR rep to discuss salary.

It's time for a true confession here: Salary negotiations are my weakness. If the job appeals to me, I tend to underbid myself just to have the opportunity to do it, and I've been a freelancer for so long, benefits seem almost as valuable as salary to me. You know you've really blown it when you name a figure and your prospective employer says, "That's exactly what I had in mind!" You probably could have gotten at least 25 percent more. That happened to me several years ago when I was hired to be the editor in chief of a weekly luxury magazine that covered L.A.'s very upscale West Side. It really was a dream job, covering fashion, film, food, real estate, design, philanthropy, fine arts, and more, but it was going to be a lot of work and I knew I wouldn't have much of a support staff. "How much is it gonna cost me to get you?" asked the brash publisher. "Um...I was thinking in the $80,000 range?" I stammered. "Done!" he cried. "When can you start?" At that point, I knew I could have gotten substantially more if I'd only named a higher figure. He was a little too willing to accept my first suggestion.

How to Negotiate Like a Hollywood Agent

Since I am obviously not a salary negotiations expert, I've pulled in the shrewdest one I know to advise you. He is of a dreaded breed—the Hollywood agent—and he is licensed to negotiate. He also happens to be my husband, and has done some killer deals for me.

James (as he's known professionally—I get to call him Jim) has his own talent agency, represents over 700 talents, and owns and operates his own sound and postproduction studio. So I'm going to humbly step aside and let him coach you on salary negotiations. In this particular area, I'm willing to share my husband with every woman out there—ladies, you're welcome to him. We're all in this together. Heeeeeeeeeeeere's Jimmy. Ooops, I mean "James."

Well, thanks, honey! And hello, everyone. First of all, let me tell you that I understand salary negotiation is a tortuous process and it's no wonder so many people wind up earning less than they might—it's really scary to press for more when you're often in the most vulnerable of situations.

So now you've been run through the mill and done the interview, the follow-up interview, met the management team, toured the office, and invested something like twelve hours of daylight and a month's worth of sleepless nights obsessing over this *great* job. And you really, really want it because if you don't get it, your landlord's going to bounce you out and the credit card goonies will come and take you away. The long-awaited call comes, they offer you a half-baked salary and tell you they'd love you to start on Monday. What do you do, what do you do, hand-wringing you? Take the gig, ya nut job! Who wants to be homeless? You can always stay safe and warm and negotiate a better deal when you've proven yourself invaluable at the office six months from now!

But for those of you who are a tad less desperate, here's the same scenario, except this time the wolf isn't at the door. Some HR rep looks you square in the eye and says, "We think we'd like to take a chance on you. The position pays $110K and comes with a generous benefits package. When can you start?"

Wow. They *like* you. They *want* you. They're offering a hell of a sweet package and it's more than anyone else ever has even considered paying you. You have worth and value to them and it makes you feel appreciated for the first time in who knows how long to hear it from what were complete strangers just a few weeks ago! So here's the most powerful negotiation technique I've ever used. And without a doubt the scariest: Don't accept. Tell them, "That's a flattering offer and I appreciate it. But it's not exactly what I had in mind. I'll think about it and get back to you."

The next several seconds of your life while you're waiting for a response may age you a few years, but believe me, there is wisdom in those lines. There's a win-win psychology behind this ploy.

First, there is a reasonable likelihood you'll get an

open-ended response such as, "Oh, is there something we haven't discussed or a concern you may have?"

You reply, "Well, I'd simply like to take a day or two to consider what you're offering."

Then they ask, "Did you have another figure in mind?"

Here's the scary part. Be polite, add 20 percent to their bottom line, and don't choke when you look them in the eye and deliver the number. You may have just earned $20K in thirty seconds.

Alternately, when you tell them you'd like to think about it, you may get a reaction such as, "Certainly [*standing up*]. Why don't you sleep on it and give me a call in the morning?"

Okay, fine. You've just informed your potential employer you're not a pushover, you feel a high level of self-worth, and you're still interested, even though you haven't yet accepted. You will call them back the next day and tell them you appreciate their offer, but were hoping for something in the range of... (20 percent more). They might be willing to negotiate, they might not. If they turn you down, then accept their original offer, knowing that you have made a lasting impression of being aware of your worth.

Then again, after you've given your "Let me think about it" response, you could also hear, "Well, frankly, I'm surprised with your reaction. We *are* talking to other candidates, but you were our first choice. When can you let us know?"

For my money, that's an egotistical bluff. The company has invested some serious time, effort, and human resources into concluding you're the best person for the job and it's very unlikely that your lack of snapping to attention on first bark is going to put them off and inspire them to show you the door.

I remember personally negotiating with a major corporation to run their entertainment department years ago. They'd made an exhaustive search over a three-month period and here they were, after rounds and rounds, actually offering me the gig. I was thrilled—it was a job I really wanted and knew it would be a valuable career peg. I turned them down twice over the course of the next several days, until we reached a package they said was their final offer and would I please let them know by morning. Naturally, I accepted the next day, pocketed a signing bonus along with a much-improved base salary, and after a champagne dinner, I slept soundly for the first time in five nights.

So be bold but be realistic. These are difficult times and you need to balance your chutzpah with the realities of your industry and your personal situation. If you decide to go for a bigger, better deal, here are a few suggestions:

1. Practice your lines. Get a friend or use the mirror and be serious about an exercise that could affect your entire career. Last time I looked, there were actually software programs out there that pitted you interactively in front of a variety of challenging hiring execs asking difficult questions on video. What a great way to prepare! You can find them in bookstores and online.

2. You're in the office and you've just been flattered with an offer you're about to negotiate. Be polite, affable, and personable, *yet firm and confident* in your response.

3. Be sure to look the point person directly in the eye when you tell them you'll have to think about it. Speak clearly and convey your response in one or two sentences. Then hold their gaze. This is your key moment of power.

4. If you sense the mood has changed because the hiring person doesn't know exactly where to take the conversation, begin to gather your things, indicating you're finished for now. You are cool, you are together, you are appreciative, and you are leaving—big smile, handshake, bye-bye, and thank you!

5. No joyous screaming, fist air pumping, or victory dances. Not until you're at least 500 yards from the commercial property. Then enjoy yourself.

Ideally, the interview and salary negotiation process will end with a celebration and sweet dreams of satisfying work and success. Occasionally, however, you'll be nagged by thoughts that something didn't go quite right—something was a little off—and you find out someone less qualified, younger, better-looking, or perhaps even related to the boss got the job offer instead of you. Do you have any recourse? The next chapter will fill you in on your options.

10

Know Your Rights (and Wrongs)

The best revenge is massive success.

—*Frank Sinatra*

I don't have to tell you that these are singularly challenging times for job seekers as well as those who are already employed. Those who have jobs are worried about keeping them, and those searching for gainful employment are distraught over intense competition for a shrinking number of positions. It seems that every week you hear a new, outrageous story about one of your peers or colleagues being laid off under what sounds like suspiciously discriminatory circumstances. Younger workers complain that they're being victimized in unfair numbers because of "last hired, first fired" policies. Those over forty feel they're losing job opportunities not only because younger workers are less expensive, but because the "out with the old, in with the new (and hot)" theory still seems applicable. It's really scary when you hear people in their early thirties complaining that they're losing out on job opportunities to the twentysomethings, and the twentysomethings complaining that there are no jobs, period. Is there hope for any of us?

Well the good news (sort of) is that at least gender discrimination is not the issue it used to be. As a matter of fact, the number of women in the workplace is on the verge of overtaking the number of men for the first time in American history. But this is not necessarily a good thing. The reason female workers' numbers are increasing is that about 82 percent of recent layoffs involved men, because men are predominantly employed in the hardest-hit industries such as manufacturing, finance, and construction. Meanwhile, more women are involved in the more recession-proof industries like education and health care. Add that to the fact that during a recession, more women go back to work because their partners' salaries are not enough, and you get a female-dominated workforce. Still, females make only about 80 cents for every dollar a male brings in, and men continue to work more hours than women because more women have part-time jobs. Those numbers apply only to nondomestic work hours, however. Surveys show that women who are employed spend much more time on childcare and domestic duties than do employed men. But looking for the silver lining, there is power in numbers, and it doesn't hurt females to be better represented in the workplace.

Another piece of good news is that age discrimination is not the issue it once was. Age discrimination filings have actually *decreased* over the past ten years. It just might seem that there are more age discrimination filings lately because: (A) Younger workers are now talking about them, and (B) if you're over forty, you're a little more sensitive to and aware of these types of cases and they're now catching your attention. These days, all age groups are being laid off and passed up. It just *seems* like the age group you're in is the worst off.

The discrimination situation has actually improved for those over forty. Remember when, back in the eighties, Jane Pauley was canned from the *Today* show because she was perceived as being "too old" at thirty-nine? Just a few years ago, when forty-nine-year-old Katie Couric left the *Today* show to become the CBS network news anchor, she was replaced by fifty-one-year-old Meredith Vieira. Age, it seems, knows fewer boundaries and limits than ever. This is partially because of sheer numbers—Baby Boomers constitute the largest group of workers in history. By 2010, more than half of the workforce in California will be classified as "older," which is defined as between the ages of forty-five and sixty-nine. There simply aren't enough younger workers to replace them all, and employers are recognizing the mature worker's value now more than ever before.

But another reason those of us past forty are not being automatically shelved for younger models is that we have redefined the aging process. How many times have you heard that fifty is the new thirty, or sixty is the new forty? Outside of the workplace, the terms "cougar" and "MILF" are considered compliments. Thanks to medical advancements that seem to be leaping forward every day, not to mention those slick little cosmetic procedures, we are more confident and look and feel younger than people our age ever have. If you want a sudden boost of youthful confidence, take a look at a photo of your mother or grandmother when they were your age. I'll bet they look at least twenty years older than you do now.

There are still some areas of concern, however, when it comes to workplace discrimination. In these tough economic times, we experienced workers need to be more aware of discrimination brought about by our higher salaries, the perceived increase in the cost of our health benefits, and our proximity to vesting in company pension plans (if any remain). We also need to be concerned about the fact that many of us need to postpone our retirement in order to make enough money to replace the savings we've lost. These factors can be held against us by current employers who are counting on us to step aside soon to make way for the newer models, and by prospective employers who need to cut their budgets.

The semi-good news is that those of us over forty have more legal recourse for age discrimination than do those who are younger. The Age Discrimination in Employment Act of 1967 (ADEA) was passed to "protect individuals who are 40 years of age or older from employment discrimination based on age." It covers both private employees and government workers. The ADEA's protection applies to both employees and job applicants and makes it "unlawful to discriminate against a person because of his/her age with respect to any term, condition, or privilege of employment, including hiring, firing, promotion, layoff, compensation, benefits, job assignments, and training."

But the ADEA is not a magic cloak that gives you protection from all perceived ageist evildoers. Take the following quiz to find out just how much the ADEA can protect you.

True or False:

1. In a job interview, it is legal for an employer to ask my age. **T/F**

2. It is legal for a potential employer to specify an age range in a job advertisement. **T/F**

3. It is illegal for my company to fire me based on the fact that I've been there the longest and am earning one of the highest salaries. **T/F**

4. If I file an age discrimination complaint, the law prohibits retaliation against me. **T/F**

5. I have no legal recourse if I am fired or demoted and my position is then filled with a younger worker. **T/F**

6. If I sue for age discrimination, I can ask for more than just wage compensation and to get my job back. **T/F**

7. It looks really suspicious if my employer fires me just before my pension vests. I would definitely have a good case. **T/F**

8. The ADEA not only protects older workers from discrimination, but younger workers as well. **T/F**

9. I'm a freelancer, also known as an "independent contractor." If an employer chooses someone younger, cheaper, and less qualified for the project, I can sue. **T/F**

10. I worked for a small company with only five employees, and was fired to make room for the boss's daughter, who was not half as qualified or experienced as I was. Under the ADEA, I have a solid case. **T/F**

11. My employer can ask me to sign an agreement to waive my rights under the ADEA. **T/F**

12. There is no longer any such thing as a legal retirement age at which I can be forced to retire. **T/F**

The Quick Answers: 1. True, 2. True, 3. False, 4. True, 5. False, 6. True, 7. False, 8. False, 9. False, 10. False, 11. True, 12. False

1. True (in some states). The ADEA does not specifically prohibit an employer from asking an applicant's age or date of birth, but some states do have laws that make it illegal to ask those questions. It's tricky, though. Because asking the question could indicate possible intent to discriminate based on age, an employer could come under legal scrutiny for asking. But let's get real here. Who among us is going to stop an interview and say, "You can't ask me that!"? Not exactly a great way to endear yourself to a potential employer. And if you wanted to prove age discrimination later, after you didn't get the job, you would have to prove that you were more qualified than any of the other candidates, which would be far more hassle than it's worth.

2. True. Employers can legally list job requirements and qualifications, even if they refer to age, in circumstances where age is shown to be a "bona fide occupational qualification" (BFOQ). For example, a clothing company can require that a model for teen fashions be within a specific age range. In the entertainment industry it's even more liberal—casting agents can request a specific age range, race, gender, hair color, weight, even breast size! If the employer can prove that an age range is reasonably necessary to the normal operation of the business, they can legally specify it in job notices or advertisements.

3. False. The ADEA does not permit you to dictate a company's hiring decisions or behaviors. Managers are allowed to make decisions about hiring and firing based on the organization's financial situation. The bitter truth is that the longer an employee has been with a company, the better the pay usually is, and the more expensive their health benefits will be to the company. It is within an employer's rights to lay off more expensive employees, as long as the decision is not made because of age, but rather salary level.

4. True. If an employer retaliates against you for officially filing a claim, it makes your case that much stronger. The ADEA makes it "unlawful to retaliate against an individual for opposing employment practices that discriminate based on age or for filing an age discrimination charge, testifying, or participating in any way in an investigation, proceeding, or litigation under the ADEA." But you must remember that once you take that step, you're never going to be as comfortable at work as you were before. You need to decide which is worth more—having the situation legally rectified and then getting the cold shoulder at work, or continuing under the adverse circumstances you're trying to eliminate.

5. False. This is why the ADEA was passed. If you can prove that your work has not eroded in any way, you can sue your employers' butts off. See the example of the workers at Saks Fifth Avenue later in this chapter.

6. True. In an age discrimination case, you may be able to ask for back pay (lost wages), front pay (future lost wages), promotion, or reinstatement to your position; compensatory damages for emotional distress; punitive damages against an employer if he/she was acting with malice or reckless indifference; attorneys' fees and court costs; and any other award that would make the victim "whole." You might also be able to force the employer to take corrective or preventive measures to ensure that the discrimination does not happen again. If you have a legitimate case, your chances of decent remuneration are actually not bad, because more jurors are likely to see themselves in a similar position someday. Everyone can relate to age discrimination.

7. False. If the employer laid you off for a legitimate reason, such as poor work performance, and can prove it, it's probably legal. If the employer laid you off because he or she didn't want to pay the benefits due, then it is illegal. It gets murky when you know you are performing your job as well as you ever have, yet you're getting lower marks on your reviews for no apparent reason. There are employers who will instruct managers to do this so they'll have a legitimate reason to lay you off before you vest. If you notice this happening, start keeping records!

8. False (sort of). The ADEA permits employers to favor older workers based on age even when doing so adversely affects a younger worker *who is forty or older.*

9. False. Sorry about that. Unless you're a full-time employee, you're on your own. The ADEA does not apply to independent contractors. Nor do sexual discrimination or harassment laws, which I found out the hard way when my editor dropped the freelance column I was writing for his publication because I wouldn't sleep with him.

10. False. The ADEA only applies to employers with twenty or more employees. But many states have laws that expand age discrimination codes to cover smaller employers. It's a good idea to look up your state's rulings on this. Although it isn't necessarily ethical, in some states mom-and-pop businesses can pretty much do as they please.

11. True. Older employees may be asked to sign waivers, releases, or agreements not to sue. This happens on occasion when the employer is offering the employee an incentive for early voluntary retirement, with a substantial amount of severance pay. You can understand why employers do this. If they're offering you a "golden parachute" in order to cut their employee costs, they don't want you coming back to sue them.

12. False. Professionals in "high policy-making positions" can legally be required to retire at age sixty-five, provided that they receive pension benefits of at least $44,000 per year. (Remember, the ADEA was passed back in the sixties when $44,000 was a high salary.)

Important exceptions. The ADEA doesn't protect everyone over the age of forty. Some noteworthy exceptions include:

- Fire and police department employees. They have their own specific physical qualifications.
- Tenured professors. Universities have the right to exercise a number of exceptional policies.
- Certain federal employees in law enforcement and air traffic control.
- Elected officials. Who are you going to file a complaint against— the voters?

- State government workers. These individuals are not allowed to sue for monetary damages under the ADEA, but can sue for "injunctive relief" to force the state to stop the discrimination.

Personally, I'm not a big fan of litigation. For one thing, it takes for-freaking-ever, and all that negative energy you expend on the legal proceedings could be invested in something positive, like learning a job skill that will help you acquire a better position elsewhere, or marketing yourself to more appreciative employers. For another thing, a lawsuit is costly. Sure, you can file a complaint for free with the EEOC, but the second you get an attorney involved, the expenses could break your bank. Still, there are instances where taking legal steps just might be worth your while. For example:

- Your boss fires you and hires a younger, less qualified employee, explaining that he wants a "fresh face" or "new blood" (or any other ageist description) in the position.

- A short while before you come into your full pension benefits, your supervisor suddenly begins finding fault with your performance, gives you negative reviews, and starts setting unattainable goals for you that other employees are not expected to reach.

- You're an executive, and the second you reach the age of fifty-five, you're shuffled off to a smaller office.

- You find that a younger worker got a promotion before the older workers even heard about the opening.

- Your boss denies you the opportunity for training courses but allows younger workers with less seniority the opportunity to take them.

- You are demoted on trumped-up poor performance charges, while a younger employee takes your place.

- Your boss turns you down for a promotion and instead hires someone from the outside who is younger and less experienced because he or she says the company needs a new image.

■ Just prior to being fired, your supervisor makes age-related remarks about you, such as that you're "over the hill," "ancient," or "ready to be put out to pasture."

If I Feel I'm Being Discriminated Against Because of My Age, What Should I Do?

First of all, you should use whatever complaint procedures are available to you through your company's own organization. Check your employee handbook for a discrimination or complaint policy, and if you can't find anything, ask someone in human resources about how to handle it. Document your reports in writing in order to create a paper trail of the discrimination. Be very specific about the nature of the discrimination, annotating dates, quotes, and whoever might have been present to witness it. You should start keeping a journal of all this, and it's best not to do it on the company computer system.

If you can't resolve the situation in house with your employer, you can file charges with the Equal Employment Opportunity Commission (EEOC), the federal agency in charge of enforcing the ADEA. Know, however, that there are very strict periods for filing charges. Usually, charges must be filed within 180 days of the alleged act of discrimination.

Your complaint must include, at a minimum, your name, address, and telephone number; the name, address, and telephone number of the party you're filing the complaint against, and number of employees if known; a short description of the alleged violation; and the date(s) of the alleged violation(s).

If it comes down to this, you can call the EEOC at 1-800-669-4000 or go to www.eeoc.gov to get details and find the location of the closest EEOC field office. You might try contacting the EEOC even if you work for a company with fewer than twenty employees, which is not covered by the ADEA. Again, different states have different laws.

Not long ago, legal options worked quite well for a couple of Saks

Fifth Avenue employees. I hate to rat on Saks, because shopping there is one of my most cherished (and rare) indulgences. I like to think of this case as an aberration, which happened only at the Bal Harbour store in Florida, when a couple of former sales associates were awarded more than $600,000 in an age discrimination suit. It seems one had been working there for eighteen years, the other for fourteen years, when their manager moved them off the sales floor and into the back room. Sales assignments to lucrative manufacturers' clothing lines were denied them and given to younger employees. The women claimed they ultimately were fired without good cause. The $600,000 award represented wage and benefit losses, liquidated and punitive damages, as well as compensation for mental anguish, loss of dignity, and intangible injuries. Last I heard, they were still negotiating on front pay, reinstatement, and attorneys' fees.

But it doesn't always have to come down to litigation. Although I love, *love* all my friends who are attorneys, I'd much rather spend time with them over dinner than over a lawsuit. My dear friend Sara Edwards managed to keep herself above the legal fray when she was unceremoniously relieved of her prominent, on-air television position. She became living proof that, in the long run, like Frank Sinatra says, **success is the best revenge**. Here's her story:

> I remember clearly the moment my safe little professional world caved in when I was forty-nine years old. It was May 2003 and I was in my twelfth year at the NBC affiliate in Boston. I was the station's full-time entertainment reporter and the movie critic for more than 200 NBC affiliates around the country. I'd covered red carpet events like the Oscars, Grammys, Emmys, and Golden Globes. The money was good, the job was good, and my contract was up. But I wasn't worried because I had built a strong following and I was an institution, wasn't I?
>
> I can still see the thirtysomething news director popping his head in my office door. "Sara, can I have a moment?" he asked rather sheepishly. I nodded and told him to make it quick, because I had to finish a story before airtime. So he

cut to the chase. "Actually, you won't be going on air tonight. We will no longer be using you."

I thought he was kidding, but he calmly persevered, offering me counseling and explaining that it was nothing personal, just a restructuring of the shows. He ended with, "Just get your things and leave when you can." I calmly walked out the door. Then I promptly called my agent and a lawyer.

I did not end up suing for age discrimination, mainly because they never replaced me with a younger model. So, with the buffer of a decent severance package, I took time off to regroup.

I smiled for family and friends... but inside I was crumbling. The relationship I was in abruptly ended. I was soon on my couch crying and stuffing my face with cookie dough ice cream. As I worked through the grief of losing my long-term job and my short-term boyfriend, not to mention my girlish figure, I decided it was time to take care of myself.

I went to the gym, redecorated my condo, adopted a cat, hung out with friends, and went to a retreat to meditate. And through all of it I learned some important lessons: I hate green tea, yoga is overrated, and surprise, surprise... I'm still Sara! TV or no TV! I also learned that my real friends couldn't care less that I wasn't that woman on the little screen anymore. I also accepted the fact that I shouldn't take being fired personally, which was not easy. But once I accepted it, I was back in action!

It took almost a year, but finally a cable network offered me a behind-the-scenes position with some reporting. But first I had to pass an interview with a larger-than-life broadcast veteran. The interview was going nicely when he threw me a curveball, asking, "Sara, you've been on air for a long time in this market, what do you think you can bring to the table at this point in your career?"

It wasn't hard to figure out he was worried that at fifty-one I was a bit long in the tooth to join their team, but I looked him straight in the eye and said, "My mother is eighty years old and has more energy than both of us combined. I have good genes, lots of enthusiasm, a wealth of experience, and can bring to the table all of my bottled-up enthusiasm and talent." I got the job.

Flash forward four years. I became the host and senior producer of a daily, hourlong entertainment show that was seen in 12 million homes throughout the eastern United States. I won four Emmys there. I mentored twentysomething reporters, and I also learned from them.

My advice for anyone staging a career comeback? Be comfortable in your own skin. Compromise when you have to, but don't sell out. Stay fit and centered. Look your best, feel your best, do your best every day. And please don't whine. Getting older sucks at times, but it's better than the alternative.

"You need to learn how to take care of yourself and your career at a time when things are broken and you feel powerless and pissed off," says career consultant and syndicated columnist Andrea Kay, who is also the author of *Work's a Bitch and Then You Make It Work*. "People often feel discriminated against when they get laid off and they have difficulty finding a new position. They want to lay the blame somewhere, and claim that it's someone else's fault, as it would be with discrimination."

Kay says that you should be aware that discrimination might not be the problem at all. "You need to take a look at yourself and understand that your problem may not be age-specific. People have perceptions, they have biases, and you can't change that. People rarely act the way you want them to, and there's nothing you can do about it. But you *can* change yourself, and you *can* change the way you influence them. Start thinking about what you can do to influence them in a different way."

That, my friends, is what a career comeback is all about. It involves assessing your wants, needs, assets, and experience, then repackaging them and presenting them in a way that will influence someone to hire you for that ideal job you've always craved. Or perhaps influence someone to invest in an idea that will take you to new professional heights. A career comeback is *not* about trying to fight against age biases and stereotypes, or forcing decision-makers to change. It all boils down to putting your freshest, most energetic and dynamic self out there in an effort to improve not only your own life, but the whole world as a result. When you're happy and prosperous, you're in a better position to pass it along. As a matter of fact, you can't help yourself. True happiness begets happiness. My professional journey took me to an extremely joyful, challenging, and satisfying place. I can't help but want to share with you what I learned along the way, so that you too can make your own dreams come true. My hopes, prayers, encouragement, and positive energy go with you. Best of luck to you all.

The Most Satisfying Work of All

People don't notice whether it's winter or summer when they're happy.

—*Anton Chekhov*

As I complete this book, I find myself at yet another career cross-roads. The U.S. economy has plummeted to its lowest level since the Great Depression. Unemployment is skyrocketing. Every day I hear reports of one more major company laying off thousands. Sara Edwards, whom you just read about in chapter 10, was laid off along with the rest of the crew when her show and almost all programming originating out of Boston were discontinued by Comcast. Nor have my own employers been immune to these difficult times. The company that hired me to manage, launch, and populate the film-oriented web-site has cut back my hours to two and a half per week—just enough to cover my health insurance, and I'm grateful to them for that. A radio station I'd been with for five years had to cut my Hollywood reports altogether. Entercom, the major radio corporation that hired me to do reports for sixteen of their stations, is still going strong, but I feel that my entertainment reports and film critiques will soon be sacrificed to the realities of shrinking radio ad revenues. Extremely savvy management seems to be pulling this company through.

My film-reporting, critiquing colleagues are losing their jobs en masse, as all media cut back and cut off. Movies and entertainment are considered part of the "fat" that everyone has been ordered to trim. I can't blame them. While Hollywood news is fun, it certainly isn't essential, and there's more than enough of it online to satisfy even the most rabid stardust addict. I can't help but wonder if the world really needs me as yet another Hollywood reporter at this point.

As I redefine my professional aspirations, I ask myself, what *does* the world really need right now? How can I make a significant contribution? While some of my professional opportunities have dried up, others are raining down. I've been blessed with numerous offers to write books, articles, television features, and more. I've been given so many opportunities, I feel the need to share my good fortune, to spread it around, to recycle and redistribute it. I don't really feel that success is mine to keep, but something to enhance and pass along.

What the world could really use right now is a large dose of hope. Perhaps, by sharing what I've learned and accomplished from my research and job search success, I can nurture some of that hope in others. Ideally, I'd love to help people pull themselves up out of the current economic mire and lead happy, optimistic lives once again. To that end, you'll see me putting a lot less emphasis on the Hollywood portion of my life, and a lot more on coaching career comebacks. For more tips and tricks and to share your thoughts, see my blog at LisaJohnson Mandell.com. I'm there for you, I'm here with you. Together we'll work our way through this current darkness, then revel in the light and share it with others. That is the most satisfying work of all.

When you're finished changing, you're finished.

—*Benjamin Franklin*

One-Day Career Comeback for $50 or Less

Now that you know all the specific details of a career comeback, it's time to get started (if you haven't already). Believe it or not, this is not an intimidating process, and can even be exciting, invigorating, and—dare I say it?—fun, if you do it right. And it doesn't have to be an expensive, laborious, months-long process. In fact, you'll be amazed at how much you can accomplish in less than twenty-four hours, after having read this book. Here's a compact program that can change your professional life in just one day.

9:00 a.m.: Spend an hour Botoxing your résumé, highlighting your special skills, and eliminating year of graduation and work experience more than fifteen years old, as recommended in chapter 8. Cost: $0

10:00 a.m.: Go for a blow-dry or style at your favorite (budget) salon. Cost: $20

11:00 a.m.: Have your makeup done in your favorite department store. At least buy a lip gloss. Cost: $10

12:30 p.m.: Return home, have a twentysomething friend or relative select a fresh, hip outfit from your closet (see chapter 4). Then have that friend snap several digital photos and help you download the best photos to your computer. Cost: $0

1:30 p.m.: Serve your photographer lunch. While you're eating, have your photographer proof your résumé. Cost: $10

2:30 p.m.: Select an elegant business card from one of the many online providers (see chapter 5). On the right sites, you only have to pay postage. Cost: $5

3:00 p.m.: Start blogging. Go on one of the many free blogging sites (see chapter 6), set up your own personal blog with a clever title that includes your specific field, post your new picture, and start writing. Make sure you add links to sites that you've found helpful. Stumped for something to say at first? Write about your one-day career comeback. Cost: $0

4:30 p.m.: Start networking! Post your gorgeous digital photo and profile, using information from your new résumé, on LinkedIn.com, Facebook.com, and any other networking sites that apply to your specific profession (see chapter 7). Find connections and friends in alumni groups, former employer groups, and special professional interest groups. Search old yearbooks and company directories for ideas about connections. Cost: $0

6:30 p.m.: Step away from the computer. Relax on the couch, kick off your shoes, pour yourself a glass of wine, or indulge yourself with your favorite treat and some mindless TV, reveling in the knowledge that you are infinitely closer to getting the job of your dreams than you were at the same time yesterday. Cost: Priceless...okay, maybe $5 for the glass of wine.

Resource Guide

Where to find the books, websites, products, and services recommended in this book

Books

Become Your Own Matchmaker: 8 Easy Steps for Attracting Your Perfect Mate. Publisher: Atria. By Patti Stanger and Lisa Johnson Mandell.

Facebook for Dummies. Publisher: For Dummies. By Carolyn Abram and Leah Pearlman.

Facebook: The Missing Manual. Publisher: Pogue Press. By E. A. Vander Veer.

Fearless Women: Midlife Portraits. Publisher: Harry N. Abrams. By Mary Ann Halpin, Nancy Alspaugh, and Marilyn Kentz.

Hollywood Beauty Secrets: Remedies to the Rescue. Publisher: Gabriel Publications. By Louisa Maccan-Graves.

How Not to Look Old: Fast and Effortless Ways to Look 10 Years Younger, 10 Pounds Lighter, 10 Times Better. Publisher: Springboard Press. By Charla Krupp.

The Huffington Post Complete Guide to Blogging. Publisher: Simon & Schuster. By the Editors of the Huffington Post.

I'm on Facebook, Now What???: How to Get Personal, Business, and Professional Value from Facebook. Publisher: Happy About Press. By Jason Alba and Jesse Stay.

I'm on LinkedIn, Now What???: A Guide to Getting the Most Out of LinkedIn. Publisher: Happy About Press. By Jason Alba.

Let's Connect: Using LinkedIn to Get Ahead at Work. Publisher: TCP Media Private Limited. By Ajay Jain.

LinkedIn for Dummies. Publisher: For Dummies. By Joel Elad.

Taking on the Big Boys: Why Feminism Is Good for Families, Business and the Nation. Publisher: The Feminist Press at CUNY. By Ellen Bravo.

Work's a Bitch and Then You Make It Work: 6 Steps to Go from Pissed Off to Powerful. Publisher: Stewart, Tabori & Chang. By Andrea Kay.

You Turn: Changing Direction in Midlife; Over 40 Stories of People Over 40. Publisher: BookSurge. By Dr. Nancy Irwin.

Products

The Carlisle Collection: Elegant professional fashions sold by personal representatives:

Mary Lin Dedeaux, AICI, CIP
Los Angeles, CA
marydedeaux@earthlink.net
www.WardrobePerfect.com

Leslie Roberts
Chicago Area Representative
Barrington, IL
leslie8486@aol.com
www.carlislecollectionbyleslie.com

Diana Stromberg
Cleveland Heights, OH
dwstrom@aol.com
www.carlislecleveland.com

Tangy Buchanan
Denver, CO
tangybuchanan@hotmail.com

Adair Keating Weiss
New York, NY
adair@goodhearts.us

Lodis: Perfect career handbags, totes, and small leather goods, available in better department stores, on Zappos.com, and at Lodis.com

Marie Monet Cosmetics: MarieMonet.com

Scribble Press: The wonderful activity venue where children (or adults) can write, illustrate, and print their own books. ScribblePress.com

Zappos.com: Super online seller of shoes, bags, and clothing of all types

Latisse: New product that helps eyelashes grow longer, thicker, and darker. Information available at Latisse.com or 1-800-433-8871

Services

Repair and updating services for all things electronic:
GeekSquad.com
FastTeks.com
GeeksOnCall.com
MakeItWork.com

Reasonable and cutting-edge Web designers:
James Richman, JamesRichman.com
AuthorBytes.com

Career assessment and guidance:
Laura McGreevy, Persprofiles.com

Photographer:
Mary Ann Halpin, MaryAnnHalpin.com

Plastic and cosmetic surgery:
Gary Motykie, MD, DrMotykie.com
Dr. George Orloff, drorloff.com

Websites

LisaJohnsonMandell.com. Find media appearances and materials, ask questions, order *Career Comeback*, or read the latest blog entry.

MichaelSantos.net. Information about Carole Santos and her husband, Michael, who earned his undergraduate and master's degrees while incarcerated.

AssessmentGoddess.com. One place where you can find access to the Self-Directed Search by John Holland and the Campbell Interest and Skill Survey.

PsychicTwins.com. Psychic Twins Terry and Linda Jamison's site offering information, services, and products.

WomenForHire.com. Tory Johnson's professional advice site and counseling services.

SmartBrief.com. Gives great information about a number of different professions, and offers several different newsletters for each.

Dooce.com. The wildly successful "Mommy Blog" by Heather Armstrong.

HollywoodBeautySecrets.com. Louisa Maccan-Graves's products, books, advice, and more.

Glassdoor.com. Find salaries of others in various fields, areas, and corporations.

Blogads.com. A service that places paid, special-interest ads on corresponding blog sites.

Technorati.com. A search engine for blogs that tracks popularity and currency.

AnotherPointofView.typepad.com. Career coach Kay Stout's well-written blog.

mymms.com. Get M&M's personalized with your message, photo, logo, etc.

Interesting News and Pop Culture Sites

HuffingtonPost.com

wowowow.com

wsj.com
nytimes.com
gawker.com
jezebel.com
thedailybeast.com
dailyfill.com

Website Template Sites

TemplateMonster.com
BuildYourSite.com
BoxedArt.com
Homestead.com
FreeWebsiteTemplates.com

Free Blog Sites (see page 118 for details)

Blog.com
Blogger.com
Blogher.com
Blogr.com
BlogSpirit.com
Blogster.com
Bravenet.com
ClearBlogs.com
LiveJournal.com
MovableType.org
Netcipia.com
OpenDiary.com
ShoutPost.com
Squarespace.com
Terapad.com
Tumblr.com
TypePad.com
Vox.com
Weebly.com

WordPress.com

Xanga.com

Yahoo360.com

Zoomshare.com

Advice for the Blogger

ChrisBrogan.com

Problogger.net

DailyBlogTips.com

Websites Where You Can Reserve Domain Names and Find Out If Anyone Else Has Them

GoDaddy.com

NetworkSolutions.com

WebHosting.yahoo.com

Free Business Card Sites

Stationary-Stationery.com

FreePrintableBusinessCards.net

Bizcard.com

VistaPrint.com

Index

Acknowledgments

I'd like to thank my husband, who had the courage to utter those three explosive words that could have ended our marriage right after it began: "You look old." It started a journey that not only revitalized my own career and image, but will hopefully help thousands more. Thank you, Jim, for supporting me, helping me, inspiring me, and loving me every step of the way.

I'm also grateful to my family: my very supportive and encouraging mother, Claire Doolittle; my sister, Karen, and her husband, Michael Foutz, who are going to great lengths to solve their community's unemployment problems by personally creating as many jobs as possible and by providing sustenance to those who are out of work. And to my amazing nieces and nephews: Rian, Jane, Devon, Aaron, Lauren, Torrie, Allie, Kami, Jacob, Luke, and baby Matthew—they inspire me to make the world a better place.

It has been a joy and a pleasure to work with everyone involved in the actual publication of this book. Karen Murgolo, vice president and editorial director at Springboard Press, is an extraordinary professional and has become a lifelong friend (I hope!). Jamie Raab, publisher, Grand Central Publishing, is one of the great ladies of publishing, and I feel honored to have her involved with my book. Matthew Ballast, executive director of publicity, went above and beyond the call of duty, and Diane Luger, executive art director, gave the book its fabulous look. Tom Hardej and Pippa White were consummately supportive and talented as assistant editors, as was Mari Okuda as senior production editor and copy editor Roland Ottewell. And of course, my gratitude is limitless for the tremendous efforts of my über-understanding and talented agent,

Eileen Cope, and her assistant, Alexandra Bicks, of Trident Media. If any of you are ever in L.A., our door is always open. Please come party with us and the golden doodle!

I'm also grateful to my cousin, Susan Merrick, along with my friends Soni Ede and Kristin Ferrand, for participating in the makeovers. You ladies were beautiful on the inside and out to begin with, and I appreciate your letting me put in my two cents. Special thanks to goddess photographer and friend Mary Ann Halpin, who made us all look and feel our best.

I have so much gratitude to all those who contributed their personal stories: Carole Santos, Chara Gavaldon, Terry and Linda Jamison, Kimberly Peterson, Pam Smallwood, Melanie Smallwood, Steve Oldfield, Patti Stanger, Lee Rappaport, Sherrill Ellsworth, Anna Nicholas, Lisa Narvas, Bonnie Laufer Krebs, Anna Barber, Darcy Pollack, and Sara Edwards.

The experts who took their valuable time to help me, including John Challenger, Dr. Nancy Irwin, Laura McGreevy, Charla Krupp, Dr. Gary Motykie, Louisa Maccan-Graves, James Richman, Denise E. Zimmerman, Ellen Bravo, and Andrea Kay, all have my extreme appreciation.

Although all my friends were supremely helpful and supportive and are greatly appreciated, two in particular seemed willing to move heaven and earth to help me with this book. They are publicist supreme Carol Berman of City Girl Media, who not only provided me with infinite media opportunities and coaching, but also with a place to crash in New York, and Susan Goodwyn Shapiro, who continues to brainstorm with me, inspire me, and cheer me on in the early morning as we walk Ali, Gabe, and KC along the L.A. "river."

About the Author

LISA JOHNSON MANDELL is an award-winning multimedia journalist and author, who never dreamed that her twenty-five-plus years of experience would be viewed as a liability by prospective employers. But she found that the precious few jobs available in film criticism and entertainment reporting were going to the young, nubile, and Internet-savvy. So she rejuvenated her image and mastered the Web to almost instantly receive myriad job offers. Johnson Mandell has been featured in the *Wall Street Journal*, on *Dr. Phil*, *Rachael Ray*, Bravo, *Forbes*, the CBS *Early Show*, NBC's *Today*, Fox News, and many other media outlets. She is a popular, international speaker, and her blog, LisaJohnsonMandell .com, is a helpful resource for all job seekers.

Lisa currently lives in Los Angeles with her husband, James, and their golden doodle, "KC." When she is not helping people land jobs they love, she's probably interviewing movie stars or preparing film reviews for media outlets such as radio stations throughout the United States and Filmazing.com.

Notes

Notes

Notes

Notes